So You Want To Be A Lawyer
A Survival Guide

Phillip Estes, Esq.

Bloomington, IN   Milton Keynes, UK

AuthorHouse™
1663 Liberty Drive, Suite 200
Bloomington, IN 47403
www.authorhouse.com
Phone: 1-800-839-8640

AuthorHouse™ UK Ltd.
500 Avebury Boulevard
Central Milton Keynes, MK9 2BE
www.authorhouse.co.uk
Phone: 08001974150

© 2006 Phillip Estes, Esq.. All rights reserved.

No part of this book may be reproduced, stored in a retrieval system, or transmitted by any means without the written permission of the author.

First published by AuthorHouse   11/20/2006

ISBN: 978-1-4259-7170-0 (sc)

Printed in the United States of America
Bloomington, Indiana

This book is printed on acid-free paper.

Table of Contents

Chapter 1
*The Lawyer **Mystique*** 1

Chapter 2
Emotionally Speaking - What does it take? 9

Chapter 3
Which College To Choose? Which Major?..................22

Chapter 4
The L.S.A.T. Exam 28

Chapter 5
A Quick Study In Law Schools 35

Chapter 6
Financial Aid: How Do I Pay For All Of This Wonderfulness? 47

Chapter 7
LAW SCHOOL: What to expect. 53

Chapter 8
Law School Curriculum & The Real World 64

Chapter 9
　　THE BAR EXAM: The Three Days from Hell. 79

Chapter 10
　　YOU'VE PASSED THE BAR: Now you're really scared! 91

Chapter 11
　　SETTING UP SHOP: Where to Begin 97

Chapter 12
　　THE LAWYER LANDSCAPE: Why the Hate? 106

Chapter 13
　　THINKING OUTSIDE THE BOX:
　　How to cultivate your practice..119

Chapter 14
　　The Rewards..137

Introduction

"The first thing we do, let's kill all the lawyers."
Shakespeare- King Henry IV - Act IV

So, you want to be a lawyer? I probably should have titled this - So, you THINK you want to be a lawyer? This is not a treatise on the law or even something to enforce what you feel the profession might hold for you. But, it is, instead, an expose' to help people understand what the law profession is and to help them decide if becoming a lawyer is really what they want to do with their lives. It is aimed at anyone - high school student, college student, law school student, someone just wanting to change careers - who is thinking about trying to become an attorney.

There are many books out there that offer advice on how to choose a law school, how to choose what type of lawyer you want to be, what law school is all about, how to pass the LSAT test, even books on how to pass the Bar Exam. But no author as of yet has specifically tried to help the potential law school student or potential lawyer address the reasons, reasoning level, or common sense of wanting to go into the law as a career. What's worse is that no author, as yet, has seen fit to help these people evaluate the market capacity of the law profession. In other words, why would anyone want to try to find a job in a particular market that was, already, overly saturated? This book specifically addresses these aspects, as well as, many other potential law career areas.

As you read this keep in mind that most of the contents are my interpretations or opinions and are based upon facts from research and events that have happened in my practice over time. And that they may or may not be applicable to your individual circumstances.

-------------------<>--------------------<>-------------------

After about two years of practicing law, I began to notice that many of the attorneys that I had dealings with were always in a bad mood. And I don't mean just a few, I mean many. It was so bad that it is almost comical. This attitude was more common with the attorneys who had been practicing less than 15 years. I became curious about this phenomenon, since I thoroughly enjoyed my practice. I began to ask them when I would see them at the court house or the local restaurants - "Are we having fun yet?" just to see what they would say. At first, I thought that perhaps it was our hard-nosed Judges. But after a few conversations, it became evident that that had nothing to do with it, because we have excellent Judges in our Circuit. The reasons behind this pervasive discontent will be discussed in more detail in some of the subsequent chapters, but it became evident that what these attorneys thought they would be doing as attorneys when they chose that career path is not what they are actually having to do in their daily practices. That fact was so very obvious. As previously mentioned, another important area that will be heavily discussed later is the current status of the market for lawyers, i.e., the old supply and demand principle. I worded it that way because, after all, practicing law is a *business* in the strictest sense of the word. And all of these people chose to get into that *business*.

As all of these people and every other lawyer can tell you, it takes a long time and a lot of hard work to become an attorney. Most people don't have the commitment or stamina to do it. It takes four years of college, then, three or four years of law school, depending upon the school and its curriculum. And, then you have to pass the bar exam which is only given twice a year. As you can see, it takes a tremendous amount of hard work. And it could take eight to ten years to accomplish! That's roughly 10 percent or more of a life time. So, with such a huge investment of time, effort, and money to become an attorney, it would be wise for a person to find out if they would like the "job" or not before starting down that path. If that person didn't check it out first and it turned out that, in fact, he did dislike the work of being an attorney, it would be doubly tragic because by then it's too late to start over in a different career.

-------------------<>--------------------<>-------------------

So, why do people choose to become attorneys anyway? A big part of the reason for people thinking that they might want to become a lawyer is what I call the *Lawyer Mystique*. We will discuss that in much more detail later, but for now, suffice it to say that the law profession is somewhat held in high esteem. And we, in the U.S., have a natural tendency to categorize our friends and associates by what they do for a living. In China, Japan, and many other cultures - age, religion, tribe, etc. are more relevant in a person's personal and societal relationships than their occupation. But here in the U.S., everyone, to some extent, relates to his fellow associates by job and we, as a society, are very comfortable with this concept. As far back as in Biblical times, when a man was referred to - he was Peter, "the fisherman." When we meet someone for the first time and begin to get acquainted with them, we will usually ask what they do for a living. If they are a bus driver, we pretty much know what they do all day. If they are an accountant, we know that they sit at a desk, wear a green visor and add numbers on an adding machine. A policeman drives a squad car and gives out tickets. In this country, we are not viewed as Jews, Baptists, widows, Democrats, etcetera, by our friends and neighbors but as teachers, secretaries, waitresses, doctors, or nurses. Conversely, it stands to reason, that when we meet someone for the first time and he tells us that he brokers intellectual property for a living, we begin to feel uncomfortable because we don't quite know what he does. A "knowledge engineer" (works with expert systems) would have a hard time getting a date because most of the ladies can't identify with what he does. If you specialize in data warehousing management, you have problems working the room at a party or, even worse, going back home for a family reunion. When I first began to practice law, relatives and friends would invariably ask me what type of lawyer I was or what was my specialty. To which I replied that I specialized in intellectual property law. This would always result in a pause and would sometimes elicit a response such as - "I didn't realize that there was any intellectual property in this part of the state." Which told me that they didn't really know what intellectual property was, but they didn't want me to know that they didn't know.

Cooks, truck drivers, teachers, or whatever - if the average guy on the street can identify with your job then he/she can be more comfortable around you and accept you as a friend more easily. Subconsciously, most everyone relates to their friends by their profession. If you meet someone for the first time and find out he's unemployed, you'll always ask what did he do or where did he work before he was laid off. We want to know so we can place them in their proper "category." My friend -the teacher; my friend - the beautician; my friend - the farmer; etcetera. Everyone feels more comfortable knowing "what" someone is/does.

Let me give you a good example of this "categorizing" concept in action. I was in the computer business before I became an attorney. I owned (and still do) a computer company (BSI) that developed a software package for hardware stores (i.e., hammers, nails, plumbing supplies) We sold computer systems and software to hardware stores in the Southeast and helped these stores with their point of sale applications. Our computer programs were tried and proven to be some of the best on the market. In the mean time, I became an attorney, but was still involved with the marketing of our software to these hardware stores. We usually had a booth hawking our software/ point of sale system at the large hardware trade shows around the

Southeast, and I would spend some of my weekends helping run the BSI booth. There was a local gentleman in my hometown, who I saw about once a week at our local post office when I would go to pick up my mail. I'll call him "Roy." He knew I was an attorney and would occasionally ask me a legal question. Well, Roy bought one of the local hardware stores, and began to manage it. About a year later, I was helping run our booth on a Saturday afternoon at the *ORGILL* hardware trade show at the Atlanta World Congress Center. Roy and two of his employees walked by. I was wearing a shirt with our BSI emblem on the pocket, and was handing out brochures for our point-of-sale (POS) system. Roy saw me and hurried over to our booth. He exclaimed "What are you doing here?" To which I replied that I owned BSI and that I was selling our POS package. He had heard of our POS system before, but he questioned me for about half an hour and he was <u>upset</u> with me. I found that quite interesting, since he thought our software package was a good package. He kept asking me - "But, I thought you were a lawyer?" "But, I thought you were a lawyer?" "But, I thought you were a lawyer?" Later, it dawned on me that I was out of my *category,* and that was what had him so upset. This happens sometimes.

-------------------<>-------------------<>-------------------

So what, exactly, does all this have to do with the law profession? Well, if someone is trying to choose a career and decides to become a mechanic, he's seen and knows what mechanics do. If, he decides to be a teacher - he's seen dozens of teachers in elementary and high school and has seen what they do. Even with Doctors, everyone has been to the doctor and seen what they do. They don't know <u>how</u> they do what they do, but they know <u>what</u> they do. Ironically, most individuals who decide to become attorneys do so based almost entirely upon false opinions of what attorneys do. What's even worse is that many people who decide to become attorneys have never even been in an attorney's office or, if they have, they do not have a clue what attorneys do. What's wrong with that picture? - " I want to become an attorney, even though I don't really know what that is, or what they do!" What are these people thinking? You, since you're reading this book, could very well fit in this group. Now, it's a given that a lot of important people are/were attorneys, but being an attorney, per say, did not make that person "important." An attorney friend of mind had just passed the Bar Exam several years ago, and I ran into him at the Court House after he had been practicing law for about six months. "What have you got going on that's important by now?" I asked. He stared back at me as though insulted and said "I'm a LAWYER! EVERYTHING I do is IMPORTANT!" I didn't respond, but I knew from his attitude that most of the cases he had signed up were menial, and he didn't want to talk about it. I, also, knew that if he kept that attitude, he would probably never have any important cases. But that is just a prime example of the ignorance surrounding the legal profession and the practice of law. This is not an isolated case. This ignorance about the law permeates from the high school level all the way through law school and, as you can see here, even sometimes, after one begins to practice law. This is the prevalent attitude of many new lawyers just starting to practice. All attorneys, who have been practicing for a year or two begin to realize that the "job" of attorney is not at all what they thought it was going to be. I call it the *lawyer myth* vs. reality.

This book is intended for high school students, college students, law school students, or anyone contemplating going into the law as a profession. It is not meant to discourage anyone from becoming an attorney, but merely an attempt - 1) to show that some attorneys do not like their work and why; and 2) to allow people to be able to make an <u>informed</u> decision as to whether the law is the right profession for them before it is too late to change their career. From my past experience with other attorneys, your decision to become an attorney will be either the <u>best</u> or the <u>worst</u> decision you will ever make, based upon your type of personality and many other factors that will be discussed later. Most of the decisions involved with this process are usually made based on false, or at best, incomplete facts relating to the law as a profession. And this book is an attempt to provide some of these little known facts to the neophyte. So, read on, my friend, and, with the help of this book you will be much more qualified to make an intelligent, enlightened decision as to your quest to become a lawyer, whether it be to reinforce your desire to become the next *Perry Mason* or to stop yourself from making the biggest mistake of your life. With that said it is time to examine this lawyer *Mystique* in depth.

CHAPTER 1

The Lawyer *Mystique*

"It is hard to say whether the Doctors of law or Doctors of divinity have made the greater advance in the lucrative business of mystery."
-- Sir Edmund Burke - Observation on a Publication.

What, exactly, is the lawyer *mystique*? Is there such a thing? We've all seen it, but we just can't quite put our finger on it. Nobody has ever defined it, and neither will I. But, *Perry Mason* had it. Johnny Cochran had it. F. Lee Bailey has it. *Ben Matlock* had it. If you've ever been in criminal court as an accused and had a lawyer to represent you, then you know what it is, but you just can't put your finger on it. When you watch the TV show *COPS* and the arresting police officer tells the "star" of the show that he has the right to an attorney, most viewers can identify with the loss of freedom that could be involved with that situation. And if a survey could be taken of the viewers at that particular point in the show, the viewers would overwhelmingly suggest that the subject ask for a lawyer. This is true even if the accused was a really *bad* criminal. The viewers all know that his chances of being treated fairly are better if he has an attorney present.

The dictionary defines *mystique* as "esoteric; having to do with things mystical; of having to do with secret rites open only to the initiated; the special esoteric skill essential in a calling or activity." This sounds very much like the word relates to a religious doctrine or rite, rather than an occupation. On the other hand, being a priest is an occupation, and priests have a *mystique* as well. One could say that attorneys are surrounded by an aura sustained by a general lack of understanding of their function in society. Although this *mystique* has existed since the time of Shakespeare or even before, I, personally, never really thought much about it until I became an attorney. I had a good friend who was an attorney that I played golf with about once a week, years ago. He was a good guy but just a bit of a stuffed shirt, so the *mystique* never surfaced with him. I had noticed it on television. And it seems that that media has always had many programs about Lawyers. I grew up watching *Perry Mason*. He always represented someone who was accused of murder and was *innocent*. He charged exorbitant fees. And he always got his clients acquitted. Many times, while Perry was cross-examining a witness, someone in the courtroom audience would stand up and shout "Stop it! Stop it! I can't stand it, anymore! Leave him alone! I did it! I did it!" This made all of the viewers want Perry for their personal attorney should they ever be charged with anything. It made for good drama but it was completely unfounded in reality. To my knowledge, no one, in the long history of jurisprudence, ever jumped up in the courtroom audience and yelled "I did it! I killed him! It was me!" Then there was Ben Matlock in his blue and white striped seersucker suits. He, also, charged outrageous fees and represented *innocent* people charged with murder. And he, too, always won his cases.

The TV networks regularly came up with new lawyer shows. *L.A.Law; the Practice; Boston Legal; Law and Order; Law and Order, Criminal Intent; Law and Order, Special Victims Unit; Law and Order, Trial by Jury*; and so forth and so on, ad infinitum. Most all of these shows about attorneys turned out to be popular and captivated our interest as a viewing public. A similar situation has arisen in the area of Criminal Justice. The Criminal Justice majors in our colleges haves increased three fold since TV shows such as *CSI* have become so popular. However, let's get real. If you want to become the next *Perry Mason* and represent *innocent* accused murderers in any small to medium sized town that you might be living in, then you are, not only, going to be extremely poor, but you are going to, literally, starve to death. First of all, in any small town there are not many murders. Secondly, if someone gets charged with murder, then they are usually not *innocent*, but guilty, and third, if someone is stupid enough to be charged with murder in the first place, then, that someone is too stupid to have enough money to pay you an exorbitant fee.

-------------------<>--------------------<>-------------------

In discussing the lawyer *mystique*, one must understand that it is a perception that, generally, applies across the board, and not just to a handful of people. If just a few people had this notion, it might be easier to understand. Perhaps, some psychology will help us to discern some of the reasons why it exists. The first psychological concept pertaining to this *mystique*, is called "stereotyping." Stereotyping is a form of *perceptual bias*. It is the "categorizing of a group into a rather simplistic mold with the simplified characteristics ascribed to the group often having no basis in fact." Usually, the stereotyped ideas of a group are widely held within a given culture and are extremely resistant to change. Stereotypes are most frequently associated with race, ethnic groups, or certain occupations. And, ironically, they are usually negative in nature but some stereotypes can be positive, as in this case. Stereotypes are very important because once they have been formed, they exert an extremely powerful influence on the individual who has formed them. We, as humans, tend to group or "categorize" to simplify a given situation. This natural tendency to simplify by categorizing is a highly useful one in that it can make certain situations we encounter in our daily lives less complex. On the other hand, it can, sometimes, cause us problems because if we use it to extremes, we can oversimplify a certain situation and even possibly omit some of the more pertinent facts. These type errors can come from 1) faulty perception, or 2) false interpretation of some or all of the components on which our stereotype is built. Many times, we will respond directly to that *category*, and may even ignore some of the more important elements of the given situation or event. As previously mentioned, much of the data perceived by the common man in building the lawyer stereotype is, for whatever the reason, faulty data.

Another concept that goes hand in hand with stereotyping is a thing called the "Halo Effect." While stereotyping generally relates to an entire category, group, or race of people, the halo effect usually applies to one individual. I first heard of the halo effect in one of the psychology courses I had as a freshman in college. Basically, according to that course, the *halo effect* refers to the initial forming of an opinion or impression of another person. Once this initial opinion has been formed in our minds, it usually plays a very *strong* role in the judgments that we, consequently, make about that individual. The phrase - "Love is blind" is an example of this concept. My first actual real life experience with this phenomenon occurred when I had been out of college for about five years. I was the project manager on a substantially large computer software installation for a Fortune 100 company. One of the systems people employed on the project was a contract systems consultant. At that time, he was the best systems professional that I had ever met and I had met dozens. He, also, was a scratch golfer. I played golf as a hobby and worked with systems for my living. This individual, who I'll call "Hank," was so good at both of these that I developed a big-time *halo effect* on him. So big in fact, I quit my job and went into business with him.

After about two years of being in business with him and my trying to decide why some of our projects lost money, it finally, dawned on me that outside of golf and computers, Hank didn't know much about anything. I had doubted my own numbers on project estimates and, even, my own judgement on some business decisions. But, I really had a hard time making myself understand that HE might be wrong about something. That thought never crossed my mind during the first eighteen months that we were in business together. I had that much confidence in him. When it finally struck me that HE might be wrong then I could see that it was HE, who had caused problems for us all along. But, it was MY fault because I was the one who had been blinded by this halo effect and had let it almost put our company into bankruptcy. I was very angry with him, but after I took the time to reflect upon what had happened and why, I understood that I was really mad at myself, because it was I who had allowed myself to be fooled. This phenomenon is very common, and the lawyer *mystique* is one form of it. When people see lawyers, they, quite often, get this "universal feeling" that effects their judgement about that person.

Supporting this view is another fact that, many times, effects us subconsciously, and that is, lots of people in positions of authority are attorneys. Just check out the U.S. Presidents. There was a stretch from 1797 until 1841, a span of some forty-four years when a lawyer was President. Of the forty-three presidents that we have had, twenty-five, or, roughly, 58 percent of them have been attorneys - some of the most famous being, Abraham Lincoln, Richard Nixon, Gerald Ford, Thomas Jefferson, and, of course, Bill Clinton. Interestingly enough, five of these lawyers did not even go to law school, namely, Andrew Jackson, Martin Van Buren, Millard Fillmore, Abraham Lincoln, and Grover Cleveland. Some of these twenty-five had additional occupations, as well, such as Jefferson, who was, also, a planter. By comparison, with the profession of attorney being the most common, the next most common profession for the Presidents is soldier. Of which, there were only five, including the likes of, Grant and Eisenhower.

The most obvious question to be pondered from all this is why there is such a big gap or disparity in the occupations of the Presidents? The occupation of Medical Doctor carries just as much, if not more, prestige as the occupation of attorney, and yet there has never been a physician elected President. One theory is that many of the people who become attorneys major in Political Science in college. Consequently, they already understand the political process and, as such, are more able to take advantage of it. Many times, this results in them running for elected office and becoming "professional politicians" instead of lawyers. And, although, a long list of former Presidential occupations might read attorney, it could be said that all of these U.S. Presidents, would have to be considered "politicians," with that having to be considered their primary stock in trade.

About four years ago, *FORTUNE* magazine ran an article on the people who had become "new" millionaires during the previous year. The number one occupation listed for the new millionaires was "musician/recording artist." The second occupation category listed for new millionaires was - you guessed it - "politician." Becoming a politician seems to be a logical step for attorneys for several other reasons as well. One being, they are used to public speaking - as they have to present arguments in open court. Many people hate public speaking. Recent studies have listed in order the greatest fears that people possess. The fear of death was the second most common phobia, while the fear of public speaking was first. So the next time you go to a funeral, keep in mind that from a phobia standpoint, the guy giving the eulogy is in worse shape than the guy lying there in the casket. And everyone knows that anytime you see a ball game on TV where the camera shows the fans, they are always scrambling for position, trying to get their face on TV. Yet, ironically, if the cameraman were to ask one of them to say a few words in front of the camera, it would put them in a complete state of paralyzed shock and panic. The fact that Attorneys do not get "stage fright" adds to the *mystique*. Furthermore, they are used to trying to persuade people to see their point of view, i.e., Judges, jurors, opposing attorneys, and they are not shy about speaking up with their opinion. All of these are traits that serve politicians in good stead. So, indirectly, it follows that as a by-product of their being attorneys, they do become "important" if they are elected to a public office such as congressman or mayor. As you can see, President is not the only elected position in which lawyers are commonly found. They exist in every post from municipal positions to the Federal level, and this helps to fan the flames of the *mystique*.

Another theory about why this happens includes the proposition that many lawyers want to change jobs. After they have been in the law profession a while and realize they don't like it, making the move to politics is an easy, slick way to bow out and not look like a failure to their family and friends. The fact that many attorneys earn notoriety through high profile cases many times gives them name recognition and helps propel them into the public eye. All of these factors grease the path to politics for lawyers. And if they lose an election they can still fall back on their practice.

-------------------<>--------------------<>-------------------

Subliminally, everyone knows some things about lawyers on a personal level that really help fuel the *mystique*. For one, they know that the person is highly educated - college degree, plus at least three years of law school. They, also, know that the person is a professional, i.e., he doesn't come home from work sweaty and dirty. Three, he/she probably makes a good income. (Most people think attorneys are rich.) Four, every time they see the lawyer he is wearing a suit. He/she is well groomed. (So far, sounds kind of like a resume for a *Husband Wanted* ad.) Five, a lawyer might have stopped someone they knew from having to go to jail. Six, he/she must be intelligent since he/she was able to pass the bar exam. And, last, the most obvious thing that happens with lawyers in everyday life that helps to foster the *mystique* is that their work almost always involves matters that are confidential. Early on, attorneys get in the habit of not discussing their work/cases with others. Even the cases that are a matter of public record are hardly ever discussed with friends or family just as a matter of course. This secrecy, once again, fans the flames.

In summary, the things discussed in this chapter have been very positive about attorneys - Professional; good income; intelligent;

Presidential material; important; even, mystical. This flies directly in the face of all the negative notions listed in the Introduction, but, in order for the proper point of view to be presented about the occupation of lawyer, both sides - positive and negative - are necessary for one to be objective. There are several chapters coming up that explain in detail many of the negative aspects of the job, but if all of the negatives were presented first, one might become discouraged and not finish reading the good stuff. I explore the lawyer's emotional make up in the next chapter. Then the next few chapters after that are intended as a guide to help prepare the potential lawyer to be an unqualified success in his/her pursuit of becoming a member of the legal profession. I will temper that perspective later with a look at what lawyers *really* do on their jobs.

Chapter 2

Emotionally Speaking
– What does it take?

"Opinion is ultimately determined by the feelings, and not by the intellect."
Herbert Spencer - Social Statics pt.iv, ch.30, 8.

  The desire to be a lawyer and the ability to be one are not related. Much of what we will discuss in the following chapters, will relate to an objective approach to the profession, but just as important, if not more so, is the subjective evaluation that each individual has to make about themselves. This chapter is designed to help you take a subjective <u>inventory</u> of your own emotional make-up to see if you are lawyer material or not.
  There are several indicative characteristics that comprise the emotional make-up of all good attorneys, and it would be wise to study these to see if you have the emotional metal to make it in the real world as an attorney. As with any study of personalities, this must be done on a case by case /person by person basis. What motivates one person many times will turn another person off. What bothers or irritates one individual is usually not even noticed by others. Some of the principles applied in psychology will help get us closer to an understanding of what the emotional make-up of a person must be in order to be able to survive in the legal arena. We've

all heard the old adage "If you can't stand the heat, then get out of the kitchen." Well, that phrase could have been written for the law profession. So, it would make sense to try to find out if you can "stand the heat" emotionally before you spend seven years and a third of a million dollars trying to get into the "kitchen," so to speak.

An honest, serious self examination on your part would definitely be in order at this point. The approach I will use here is to offer a list of questions and answers with extensive explanations of each. You should ask yourself each of these questions and answer them honestly before reading the answers and clarifications of each, to see how well you score from an emotional aspect on these points. If you fail to score a good grade, you should seriously reevaluate your desire to go into the law as a career, since all of these things will become important issues or at least considerations in your future practice. Simply put, one MUST have the proper temperament to be an attorney. Even, if the previous reasons I have given didn't dissuade you, if you are not cut out to be a lawyer *emotionally* then you can't be one happily or successfully. So, for your own sake, you MUST realize that only certain individuals have the required *disposition* to become successful lawyers.

The following set of questions are provided for you to test yourself with regard to your emotional make-up. So, get a piece of paper and pencil, read the questions and answer them honestly, as this will result in an extremely good indicator of your ability to withstand the emotional roller coaster that is the law. On the questions that ask for a yes or no answer, don't hedge and say "Well, it depends." Be honest, and answer which is true most of the time for your personality. Here goes:

1) Do you get your feelings hurt easily?

2) Does it bother you for someone to question your work?

3) Do you like arguments or do you tend to avoid them?

4) Does it bother you to have to give a speech to a group?

A Survival Guide

5) Would you be comfortable in a job where you might go two to three months without a paycheck?

6) Do people say you have a short temper?

7) If the Court appointed you to represent an indigent (poor) person who had already been in prison a couple of times, and he told you that the charges were true - that he had, in fact, raped and sodomized his 12-year-old neighbor, - could you represent that person with true zeal?

8) Do people say you cry easily? Do you cry when you get mad?

9) Once you became a lawyer would you tell a potential client that you thought they had a "good" case just to get the business, even though you knew it was a big "loser" with no chance of recovery, if his fee was the *only* chance that you had to keep from getting kicked out of your law office that afternoon for nonpayment of rent?

10) Do you work well under pressure or does it tend to make you nervous?

11) Since you became an adult, have you ever become "upset" because someone (husband, boss, store clerk) was *mean* to you?

12) Would you tell a judge the truth in Court, knowing that by so doing you would be put in jail for 24 hours for contempt of court, even though the chances were 99.9% that no one would find out if you told the Judge a lie to avoid jail?

13) Are you well organized at home, school and/or work?

14) Have you been in a fist fight as an adult?

15) Have you ever been convicted of a felony?

16) Do you think marijuana should be legalized?

17) Are you easily discouraged when things don't go your way?

18) Do you procrastinate - put things off until the last minute?

19) Do you enjoy reading?

20) Do you feel stress can damage a person's health?

21) Do you or have you ever worked or gone to school with someone who really gives you a hard time and you desperately wished that they would stop? Or this person actually caused you to change jobs?

22) Do you have a tattoo?

23) Do you use recreational drugs?

24) Do you have good self discipline?

------------------<>--------------------<>------------------

The questions will now be listed first, then the <u>most</u> appropriate answer for emotional stability as it applies to the legal profession, followed by an analysis of just why the given answer is correct.

1) Q: Do you get your feelings hurt easily?

A: NO. The ability to remain objective and not allow your feelings to become a part, much less a large part, of your work is very important. While practicing law you will be bombarded on a DAILY basis with insults, comments about your honesty and ethics, lawyer jokes, lawyers as scum bags in general. There are millions of lawyer jokes and you will hear every one of them from your friends during the first year or two of your practice. If this doesn't sound appetizing to you then do us both a favor and move on to a different line of work.

2) Q: Does it bother you for someone to question your work?

A: NO. Keep in mind that the Law is extremely technical with very strong emphasis placed upon following certain procedures to the letter. You can lose a case, be sued for malpractice, even, possibly, be disbarred if you do not strictly adhere to the given required procedure for that type of case. So, although I am diligent and meticulous in my work, I am, also, human and make an occasional mistake. Not only does it not bother me for a clerk in the court clerk's office to peruse my work, I really appreciate it when they catch a mistake that I or one of my staff has made. The opposing attorney on a case will, also, examine your filings (work) closely and really embarrass you if you make a mistake on something sent to him/her. So if you are uncomfortable with someone questioning your work or second guessing you, then please <u>move</u> on.

3) Q: Do you like arguments or do you tend to avoid them?

A: YES. When growing up, if you engaged your siblings, mother, and father, in occasional arguments just for fun then you might be lawyer material, especially if you usually won. If you avoid arguments and let the other side have their way just to avoid a confrontation, then probably not. In practice, you will be confronted on a DAILY basis with arguments from the judge, your clients, opposing legal counsel. You need to love to argue, not just like it but love it. If you don't, please, <u>move</u> on.

4) Q: Does it bother you to have to give a speech to a group?

A: NO. In practice you will be performing public speaking on an almost DAILY basis. You will be required to think on your feet and answer difficult, intellectually stimulating questions in front of hundreds of people at times, with your answers being heard and scrutinized by everyone in the room. If you mispeak you could - cost yourself jail time for contempt, cause a mistrial, or even lose your clients case whereby he/she could go to prison or lose thousands of dollars, resulting in your being sued for malpractice. If you are <u>not already volunteering</u> to give presentations or to be the spokesperson for your group then that shows a reluctance on your part to this type of activity, so - you guessed it - <u>move</u> on.

5) Q: Would you be comfortable in a job where you might go two to three months without a paycheck?

A: YES. Keep in mind that most people are used to getting a regular paycheck. Are you? And if you have a family to support, then things like the pressure of clients who bounce checks, the over crowded lawyer market, State Treasurer not paying on time for indigent work because of budget proration, etc. could be more than you could stand. Think about it and <u>move</u> on.

6) Q: Do people say you have a short temper?

A: NO. Cool heads must always be prevalent in the legal arena. If you lose your cool, and I mean just once, in front of the Judge then you will be a marked man, not to mention possibly being held in contempt. The opposing attorneys at trial go at each other as though they could kill each other and then when the Judge calls noon recess, they go to lunch together. To outsiders it appears that they hate each other when in reality they are probably fast friends. They can control themselves emotionally enough to present whatever the situation dictates. If you get angry in court and lose your cool, you cause everyone problems, most of all yourself. <u>Move</u> on.

7) Q: If the Court appointed you to represent an indigent (poor) person who had already been in prison a couple of times, and the subject told you that the charges against him were true - that he had, in fact, raped and sodomized his next door neighbor's 12 year old daughter, - could you represent that person with true zeal?

A: YES. Once again, we must keep our emotions out of this. The State pays these court appointed, indigent attorneys to represent these poor, accused people and to do it diligently. Our justice system is not set up to be swayed by emotion on anyone's part. The law says that the person is innocent until PROVEN guilty. You are getting paid to force the D.A. to prove that this person actually did it. You are not getting paid to determine guilt. So you MUST provide your client with your greatest effort and zeal in your representation of him. Now, let's look at the other side of the coin. It's interesting to see just why the legal system must work the way it does. For argument's sake, let's say you became influenced by your emotions and actually helped get him convicted to 25 years in prison for these crimes and, at the end of the day, felt good with your contribution to society by helping get this scum put away. Fast forward - two years later you are in the check out line in at the grocery store and he comes up to you, confronts you and calls you every name in the book. You begin to wonder just how did he get out? When you arrive at your office the next day you go on the State's web site and search for his name. Sure enough, he has an appeal in there. It reads like this.

> State of Alabama v. M.N.S.
> Defendant, MNS, was convicted for Rape II and Sodomy II and sentenced to 25 yrs. Appellant appealed. Evidence was never presented to the Court that Appellant was mentally incompetent when not on his medication *Zyprexa*, a very strong psychotic drug. MNS was not given his medication while incarcerated before trial and was in an hallucinating state from time to time without it. He confessed to the charges while not in a lucid state, and was sentenced. DNA evidence from a rape kit from another child who was raped ten months later proved that MNS was, in fact, not the one who had committed the crime. Overturned. See just how one's <u>emotions</u> can cause severe problems in the legal arena!

8) Q: Do people say you cry easily? Do you cry when you get mad?

A: NO. NO. If you cannot control your emotions well enough to keep from crying at times, (and I don't mean at funerals), then you are not emotionally stable enough to be able to be an attorney, except to work in a clerical setting such as a civil service/social security administration type position where public contact is limited to letter correspondence. If things get hot and heavy in Court and you start crying then you are in deep trouble with the Judge, your client, and, most of all the jury. Move on!

9) Q: Once you become an attorney, would you tell a new potential client who just walked in off of the street that had a "real loser" case that he had a "good" case, if that was the <u>only</u> way you were going to be able to have the money to keep from being evicted from your office that afternoon for none payment of rent?

A: NO. You can't be changing from objective to subjective and back, in situations such as this. The ability to possibly get the money from somewhere else that afternoon, talk the landlord into an extension, or find another suitable office is still with you. The ability to keep this new client from worrying you to death and causing you to get an ulcer or at best many, many sleepless nights, is not still with you. These scenarios occur much too frequently in the legal profession today. Sometimes, attorneys find themselves so strapped for cash that they begin to accept cases that have no merit and wind up with extremely bad morale as a result. They forget that even the best lawyer that every lived can't make chicken salad out of chicken shit. <u>Move</u> on.

10) Q: Do you work well under pressure or does it tend to make you nervous?

A: YES. If job pressure and/or other types of pressure tend to stimulate you and help keep you motivated then you might have the proper attitude toward pressure to be able to handle the situations of the attorney job. Whereas, if you get "flustered" and have trouble maintaining your composure under pressure then you are going to have big problems in court. The amount of nervousness that you have already encountered in your high school activities such as exams, speeches, and SAT tests will give you a very good indication of just how you will do. How nervous would you be if forced to take a big test that you had never studied for? Does pressure make your hands shake sometimes? How are the Judge, jury, and your client going to feel in court when they see your hands shaking nervously? You say that you are not going to be a Courtroom lawyer - that you are going to only take cases that don't require going to court. Well, guess what? Just about any case that you take can turn sour and wind up in court! Nervous? Well, <u>move</u> on.

11) Q: Since you have become an adult, have you ever become "upset" because someone (husband, boss, store clerk, girlfriend) was <u>mean</u> to you?

A: NO. We all know that we have absolutely no control over the behavior - good or bad - of our peers. Nor do we have any control over what they say. Since we can't control what other people say to us, about us, or against us, and if we interact with the public on a regular basis then it follows that eventually someone is going to say something we don't like - something really *mean* to us. If we can't control what other people say and/or do unless we're their boss then we are left with the option of liking what someone else says about us or lumping it. However, we *can* control how we react to what someone says. If you can't be told by someone else - make that *anyone* else - that something about you stinks without it "upsetting" you then <u>move</u> on.

12) Q: Are you well organized at home, school and/or work?

A: YES. If you presently find yourself spending a lot of your time looking for stuff that you've misplaced or can't find, then your ability to be a successful attorney is seriously in question. When you begin to practice, you will be handling very important documents on a daily basis. If you realize that you can't find a client's file, it could be that you've misplaced a deed, a will, or some other very important document that will be *impossible* to replace. Does this really sound like fun to you? Believe me it's not if you're unorganized. <u>Move</u> on.

13) Q: After you begin to practice, would you answer truthfully in court, with the knowledge that by so doing you would be put in jail for 24 hours for contempt, even though the chances were 99.9% that no one would find out if you told the judge a lie to avoid jail?

A: YES. One night in jail is a small price to pay to keep your integrity intact. Once you breach that, it will become easier and easier to compromise the truth. Usually, in the situations like the one described above the judge will be lenient if the lawyer is truthful. But if you lie and it is ever found out, the judges will all hear about it and put you on their subconscious "liars' list." Not good. <u>Move</u> on.

14) Q: Have you ever been in a fist fight as an adult?

A: NO. The reason we have assault laws is to keep people from fighting. You should always call the police if you find yourself in a situation where you need to be protected, instead of fighting.

15) Q: Have you ever been convicted of a felony?

A: NO. The state bar where you live will perform an intense background check on you when you apply to take the bar exam. If you have a prior felony on your record you cannot be an attorney. You have no say in this. It is absolute. <u>Move</u> on.

16) Q: Do you think marijuana should be legalized?

A: NO. Marijuana is an illegal drug. If you feel it should be legalized then you believe strongly in something that is illegal. Your mind set is not proper to be a good criminal or even, civil advocate. How much damage will it do your practice to get your name in the newspaper for being arrested for drugs? You may think "Well, lots of people think marijuana should be legalized. I could get them to be my clients." The problem with that logic is that NO ONE wants an attorney to represent them that they suspect might be using drugs. <u>Move</u> on.

17) Q: Are you easily discouraged when things don't go your way?

A: NO. In most court cases, there are usually one winner and one loser. Very seldom does the outcome of a case result in both parties winning. Therefore, statistically speaking, even if you are an excellent attorney, you will lose about half of your cases. You can't win 'em all. If you get discouraged easily when things go against you then you will spend a lot of your time in law practice discouraged and/or unhappy. The National Institute of Mental Health says that, on average, *9.5 % of American adults suffer from a depressive illness and for lawyers that number is almost doubled.* In other words, approximately 20% or one in five of all American lawyers suffer from depression. Do you want a job that takes so much expense and effort to get, to just be depressed all of the time? <u>Move</u> on.

18) Q: Do you procrastinate or put things off until the last minute?

A: NO. Your ability to do a good job at managing your time and that includes not putting things off, is crucial to having a successful law practice. There will be many, many issues that will come along in your practice that will be beyond your control that will disrupt the smooth flow of your work. Added to that, having things that disrupt the smooth flow of your work that you bring upon yourself will, at times, become more than you can bear. Many of the things lawyers deal with - appeals, tort lawsuits, answers, - have deadlines that must be adhered to in order to be valid. If you put things off until the last minute and, say, your computer breaks down that morning then there is a good chance that you will miss one of these deadlines, and be forever barred from filing the action that you were attempting to file. Not good. <u>Move</u> on.

19) Q: Do you enjoy reading?

A: YES. There is probably not another job out there, unless perhaps one in editing, that requires more reading than does legal work. Even with the help of the excellent internet research tools that we have available to us today, lawyers still have to spend a tremendous amount of time reading. And the things that we have to read are always very technical and usually not at all interesting. So, if you don't already read more than you watch TV then <u>move</u> on.

20) Q: Do you feel stress can damage a person's health?

A: NO. The function stress plays in a person's overall being varies greatly from individual to individual. Stress in most situations causes adrenalin to be released into the bloodstream. Fight or flight syndrome occurs in many cases through this chemical mechanism and can save a person's life in the right situation. In job situations it can either hurt or help the person experiencing the stress. Stress occurs when the time is running out at the end of a close basketball game and this adrenalin rush allows the athletes to perform at their highest level. However, in an office setting, many times stress can be counter productive. Most people don't like to be placed in stressful situations, while others need an occasional stress inducing event to operate at their maximum efficiency level. If you fit in the first category here then the law is probably going to be too stressful for you, and you need to move on. If you fit, as I do, in the second group then you will be OK in that area.

21) Q: Do you or have you worked or gone to school with someone who really gives (gave) you a hard time, and you desperately wish(ed) that they would stop? Or, maybe, they even caused you to change jobs?

A: NO. In practice you will be dealing with obnoxious, offensive, vile, unsavory, despicable people on a DAILY basis. But, as an attorney, you must approach your job with the same attitude that Charles Dickens proclaimed when he once said "If there were no bad people, there would be no good lawyers." These kinds of people will always be around and if you can't deal with them then you need to become a housewife or househusband, whichever the case may be.

22) Q: Do you have a tattoo?

A: HA. I put that one in there just to get your attention. Having a tattoo does not affect your law ability one way or the other. However, keep in mind that having a tattoo on a visible skin area will let clients, Judges, and the other lawyers know that you've been *drunk* at least once.

23) Q: Do you use recreational drugs?

A: NO. When you become an attorney using drugs will never be an option for you. So if you use drugs now, then you need to move on, because you've already missed your chance.

24) Q: Do you have good self discipline?

A: YES. Self discipline is one of, if not, the most important aspect of the attorney's personality, his/her ability to be able to *control* himself/herself in almost any situation. This is the reason that you don't see many "fat" lawyers practicing law.

------------------<>--------------------<>-------------------

Well, how did you do? I suppose some of you won't even read the rest of this book since I've presented all of these negative things about your personalities. Seriously, for those of you who did not score well on these, I strongly recommend that you think twice about whether becoming an attorney will make you happy in the long run. These questions are very much on point for what you can expect to have to deal with when you begin to practice law. Therefore, if your personality doesn't present the characteristics that are needed, then you probably won't be able to learn to like most of the negative things listed. And if you are one of the ones that have just decided maybe it's not right for you, I wish you would drop me an E-mail and thank me for saving you so much time, money and effort in a pursuit that was not meant for you anyway. Hey, look at it this way. Guys go into criminal justice and study forensic science thinking that they are going to be the next *CSI* expert. But they wind up trying to keep from throwing up while having to clean up the blood and guts after a triple homicide/suicide. Ladies go into nursing thinking they are going to help sick people get well, work hand-in-hand with the world's best physicians, and have a great career in medicine. Then, they start on their job and get stuck with giving enemas, changing bed pans, and constantly trying to avoid catching AIDS from the patients. So, it could be worse. It's better that you found out now instead of eight years from now when it's too late to change your career. I wish you good luck with your future. Now, on to something a little more positive.

CHAPTER 3

Which College To Choose? Which Major?

Training is everything. The peach was once a bitter almond; cauliflower is nothing but cabbage with a college education.
Mark Twain -   Pudd'nhead Wilson. Chap. 5

As I said in a previous chapter, there are many reasons for choosing to go to law school. The reasons that people have for wanting to go into law as a profession are as varied as the people themselves. They may want to save the world; to save humanity; to save our freedoms; to save the dolphins; to keep innocent people out of jail; to keep guilty people out of jail; to be the next *Perry Mason;* to make a million bucks; and so forth. The reasons range from mild to wild. What many of these people don't realize is that some of the decisions they make as early as junior high or high school can have a profound impact upon their chances, at a later time, of getting into a good college, law school, and/or even their ability to pass the bar exam. Most books giving advice on law school prep emphasize the importance of your choice of a college and your college GPA. Well, just as important to you, career wise, is your choice of what major you pick. What you choose as your major has a huge impact on how your career will shape up. Law schools don't really place much weight in which major you chose, unless it is in an area such as physical education, coaching, music, recreation, or something similar As you can imagine, these type majors will not serve you as well as some others that you could choose, but, just about anything else - history, math, accounting, business, biology, even literature, will do fine. There were several students in my law school class who were nurses and we even had one high school teacher. They all did very well.   Law schools need students who are critical thinkers and can be independent. College courses that help develop the ability to think logically and to be able to *write* intelligently and with authority are very good choices, also.

Let's start our discussion of this, with a good example of what I'm talking about. I have a relative who is an attorney and he practices in New Orleans. He was older than me and I rarely saw him when I was a teenager, as he had already graduated from college. He and I have discussed the law profession at times at family reunions and at occasional funerals for a family member. His undergraduate grades were excellent and he attended the Tulane School of Law and eventually, was admitted to the Louisiana Bar. He was quite a contrast from me, since I didn't start to law school until I was in my thirties. He hinted, after he found out that I was in law school, that he wished that he had majored in accounting, like I did rather than Political Science. I was rather surprised when he told me this because he was generally recognized by the family as our "shining star," and even more surprising was the fact that, by then, he had already been practicing for about 20 years.   You see, political science courses do very little to prepare someone for the Law School curriculum, and many with that major have their practice turn out to be a "general practice" instead of being able to offer a specialty such as patent law, etc. When potential clients walked into my relative's law office with a case they didn't ask if he made all "A"s or even which school he went to, but, rather, could he help with their problem? Having a major in something like accounting could have aided him in helping more of these potential clients than the Political Science major did. I soon realized that Political Science is the major of choice for many planning to go to law school after college graduation. Many colleges offer an undergraduate major called "Pre-Law" which, in essence, is just a glorified name for political science.

Many of the people who went to law school with me majored in Political Science, But, just how smart is that? Now don't get me wrong. Political Science is good. Political Science is fine. But, as you will see, it has its limitations. Let's take the case of a young man from my hometown who graduated from my law school about two years before I did. I'll call him "Dan." He majored in Political Science at one of the local universities. When I went down to Montgomery to take the Bar Exam, I ran into "Dan" who was, also, taking the exam. That was his *fifth* time to take it. (I knew he had flunked it four or five times already and I saw him in the rest room while we were on break on the second day of the exam. I asked him - "Hey, Dan. You ever think that maybe it's not the **test**?!") Anyway, I checked the Bar registry for the next three or four times the exam was given, and he was not listed as having passed. He took the Bar exam eight or nine times and failed it every time! What career options does "Dan" have available to him at this point? With political science as his major, he is very, very limited. If he had majored in accounting or even nursing, his future would be much brighter now. He can't even get a job teaching with a political science major, because he would need a teaching certificate, as well. The point I'm trying to make is that the very slight advantages that a major in political science might give you in law school are far outweighed by the disadvantages of not having a more useful, professional undergraduate degree. Law schools require a bachelor's degree to be admitted, but usually have very few limitations upon the choice of major that a potential student must have. So, in the overall scheme of things, basically, it's up to you to make your best choice of a *major* for yourself.

Most students looking forward to becoming a lawyer don't want to consider the possibility of not being able to pass the bar exam, but, it happens. If you don't believe me, just ask "Dan." One lady in my law school class, (I'll call her, Lucy) took the exam seven or eight times before she passed it. She was almost ready for the insane asylum by then. And, if you do pass the bar exam, having a professional type of degree could be a huge help in your law career. For instance, it will take you four years and a lot of money to get a B.S./B.A., which is required for you to be admitted to law school. So depending on which major you chose for your BS/BA, when you become an Attorney, you could be a lawyer and an accountant, a lawyer and a computer scientist, even a lawyer and a chemist - or you could be just a lawyer if your choice of undergraduate major is weak. Spend some time researching the different majors. Get on the Internet or use whatever other research tools that you might have available and do your homework before choosing. Selecting a subject that you already enjoy is usually a good choice, and remember that statistics show that over 90 percent of all college students change their major at least once before graduating. So, don't stop checking it out just because you've found something you like. Use a little common sense in your decision - *Basket Weaving* may be an enjoyable major, but it won't get you very far in the law school admission process or in your career.

You might, also, consider the fact that you will be there for four years and you could get a double major if you like and are willing to apply yourself. A double major usually doesn't take any longer to get than just a regular major, if you work your electives toward that end. My wife, my niece, and myself all have double majors. My wife's are Biology and Lab Technology; my niece's are English and Journalism; while mine are Math and Accounting. This can be very beneficial to you in your career. For instance, let's say you choose to major in Chemistry and Accounting. The Chemistry major will qualify you to apply to become a Patent Attorney once you've passed the Bar, while the Accounting will allow you to read and understand your client's financial statements, and your firm's, as well, for that matter. It would, also, qualify you to sit for the CPA exam - no small feat in and of itself. A patent attorney, who was, also, a CPA would truly be armed and dangerous. Of course there are some other things that you have to do besides just take and pass these exams in order to complete these different certifications, but choosing majors that qualify you to be a professional gives you a big advantage in being a true professional.

---------------------<>--------------------<>------------------

Another area that is just as important, if not more so, is the choice of a college for your undergraduate degree. This could be an important item on your law school application and eventually your resume. There are many, many options available. But, unless you have some type of financial aid, a scholarship, or rich parents you may want to look into going the community college route for your first two years. I have taught at several community colleges during my career and I have found them to be a very viable option for a college student's first two years. Keep in mind as you start your college career that if you intend to stick with your dream of becoming a lawyer, it is going to be seven or eight years and many, many thousands of dollars. Most community college courses transfer directly to the university of your choice and the cost is less than half what the major universities cost. The money you could save might help to cover the cost of law school, later. Grades are also a major consideration, as your GPA needs to be as high as possible for your law school application. So, attending a community college for two years could get your GPA jump-started. I've found that at the four year universities, many times, first and second year students will get stuck with professors who also teach in the graduate programs. And these teachers sometimes have a tendency to talk over the students' heads. Additionally, these instructors will be more "ivory tower" in their approach to teaching and research, and in many instances the freshman student's grade will suffer because of this. This can be especially true if the teacher is a department head and/or already has tenure. On the other hand, this is very, very rarely the case at a community college. There the faculty is more student - as opposed to research - oriented. These grades will transfer and give you a tremendous head start on your GPA. Remember, also, that the diploma shows the name of the college where you *finish*, not the name of the college where you *start*. In addition, taking classes at two different colleges helps break the monotony that you sometimes get when going to a four-year school. I know, because when I was an undergrad, I went to Jacksonville State University and, also, spent two semesters at the University of Alabama in Tuscaloosa - one in my sophomore year and one in my senior year. I didn't do this just for the change of scenery, but, believe me, it really helped to break the monotony of going to the same school for four straight years. The two schools' atmospheres, culture, and experience were very different and very enlightening.

Get involved with the student government association. Also, sign up for the debate team. This is very good practice for you to learn to think on your feet. If your school offers classes in theater or has a drama department then give that a shot as well. Becoming a good actor can bode well for you in the courtroom, plus these types of activities will help you to be a better public speaker and not get stage fright so easily. They look good on your law school application, too.

As was explained earlier, with the major you pick, the school you choose could, also, help or hurt your chances in your admission to law school, so, be sure to pick a college that is accredited. Other factors, besides accreditation, such as cost and location should be explored, as well. Picking one that is in your state of residence will save you a considerable amount of tuition unless you have a scholarship. Obtaining a college catalog from each school, either online or by mail, very early in your selection process will help you tremendously. In the next chapter we will skip forward to the Law School Admissions Test, more commonly called the LSAT. If you are just now starting to college it will be three years before you take this test, so you may want to wait until closer to the time to take the test to study this next chapter, but it won't hurt for a quick run through now.

Chapter 4
The L.S.A.T. Exam

Only those who dare to fail greatly can ever achieve greatly.
Robert F. Kennedy

There are 220 law schools in the United States. Of which, 180 are accredited by the American Bar Association. Whether accredited or not, almost all of these require their applicants to take the Law School Admission Test (LSAT). So, you will have to register and take this test in order to be admitted to the law school of your choice. The scoring requirements on this exam vary from school to school, but the test is *required* for you to be considered by them as a potential student. The organization that administers the test is the Law School Admission Council (LSAC). It is a nonprofit corporation that has most of the law schools in the U.S. and Canada as members. LSAC offers a number of specialized services for these schools to facilitate the law school admission process. All of these law school admission assessments and decisions are made by individual law schools using a combination of each school's own admission procedures and the information that LSAC collects for each applicant's file. Not all law schools utilize the LSAC's services but almost all utilize the LSAT test scores in their screening process.

The LSAT test is a standardized, half-day test given four times each year at predesignated testing centers throughout the world. All

LSAC-member schools require law school applicants to take the LSAT. The LSAT is designed to measure skills considered necessary for success in law school, namely: the reading and comprehension of complex texts with accuracy and insight; the organization and management of information and the ability to draw reasonable conclusions from it; the ability to think critically; and the analysis and evaluation of the arguments of others.

The test consists of five 35-minute sections of multiple-choice questions. Four of the five sections contribute to the test taker's score. These sections include one reading comprehension section, one analytical reasoning section, and two logical reasoning sections. The unscored section typically is used to pretest new test questions. The placement of this unused section, which is commonly referred to as the variable section, varies among the different test centers and testing dates. A 35-minute writing sample is administered at the end of the test. LSAC does not score the writing sample, but copies of it are sent to all law schools to which a candidate applies.

The most efficient way to register for the test is to go to www.LSAC.org and establish your online account. This will accomplish several things for you. First, it will enable you to print out your LSAT ticket instead of waiting for it to be mailed, and you will be able to get your LSAT score early via e-mail. You can complete all of your transactions online once you set up an account, and you will be able to keep track of your entire file online. A valid credit card is required to be able to register for the test or for other online services.

------------------<>--------------------<>------------------

Law School Data Assembly Service (LSDAS)

The LSDAS provides a means of centralizing and standardizing undergraduate academic records to simplify the law school admission process (for U.S. Law Schools only). Canadian law schools do not participate in the LSDAS and do not require its use. The LSDAS prepares a report for each law school to which you apply. There is a registration fee for the LSDAS, as well as a fee for each law school to which you apply.

The law school report contains information that the schools use, along with your application, personal essay, letters of recommendation, and other criteria, to make their admission decisions. Information contained in the report includes:
. an undergraduate academic summary
. copies of all undergraduate, graduate, and law/professional school grade transcripts
. LSAT scores and writing sample copies
. copies of letters of recommendation processed by LSAC.

---------------<>---------------<>---------

LSAC contact information:

By mail:
Law School Admission Council
622 Penn St
Box 2000
Newtown, PA 18940-0998, USA

By the internet:
www.LSAC.org

By e-mail:
LSACINFO@LSAC.org

By fax:
215.968.1119

By phone:
215.968.1001

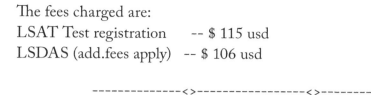

The fees charged are:
LSAT Test registration   -- $ 115 usd
LSDAS (add.fees apply)   -- $ 106 usd

---------------<>-----------------<>--------

<u>The LSAT Test</u>

There are many books and publications available to help you prepare to score well on the LSAT, and buying at least one of these would be money well spent. Most law school applicants familiarize themselves with the types of questions presented on the test, and the test directions beforehand. Taking several practice tests is also recommended. The application booklet furnished by the LSAC has several sample tests in it that you can take.

The test is composed of the following:
. Reading Comprehension Questions
. Analytical Reasoning Questions
. Logical Reasoning Questions
. The Writing Sample

------------<>-----------------<>--------------

- Reading Comprehension Questions

The reading comprehension questions are designed to measure your ability to read, with understanding, examples of lengthy and complex materials similar to those commonly encountered in law school work. The reading comprehension section of the test consists of four passages, each about 450 words long, followed by six to eight questions that test your reading and reasoning abilities. Texts for these questions come from the sciences, humanities, law, and social sciences.

Reading comprehension questions require you to read carefully and accurately, to determine the relationships among the various parts of the passage, and to draw reasonable inferences from the subject matter presented. The questions may ask:

- The main idea the passage presents
- The meaning or general purpose of the words in the passage
- Information that can be inferred from the passage
- The organization of the passage
- The information explicitly mentioned in the passage
- The correlation of passage subject matter to a new context
- The tone of the passage or the author's slant as it is revealed in the language used.

- Analytical Reasoning Questions

The purpose of analytical reasoning questions is to measure your ability to understand a structure of relationships and to draw logical conclusions about the structure. You are asked to make deductions from a set of statements, rules, or conditions that describe relationships among entities such as persons, places, things, or events. They simulate the kinds of detailed analyses of relationships that a law student must perform in solving legal problems. The text used for each group of questions describes a common relationship such as these:

- Queuing theory: B arrives before C, but after D;
- Grouping: seven computers are networked together - L,M,N,O,P,Q, & R - which can pass data to which?
- Spatial: a subway system has eight substations and some of the trains are one way, etc.

Keep in mind while attempting to solve these type problems that some of the relationships are fixed, while others are variable. No formal training in logic is required to answer these questions correctly. They are intended to be answered using knowledge, skills, and reasoning ability found at the college graduate level.

- Logical Reasoning Questions

Logical reasoning questions are designed to evaluate your ability to understand, analyze, and complete a variety of arguments. The arguments are contained in text taken from various sources, including advertisements, commercials, newspapers, debates, discussions and conversations, as well as articles in the humanities, the social sciences, and the natural sciences.

Each logical reasoning question requires you to read and comprehend a short paragraph, then answer one or two questions about it. The questions test a variety of abilities involved in reasoning logically and thinking critically. These include:

. recognizing the point or issue of an argument or conflict;
. detecting the assumptions involved in an argument or chain of thought;
. identifying and applying principles;
. identifying the structure of an argument or chain of reasoning;
. drawing reasonable inferences from certain given evidence;

The questions do not require you to know any of the vocabulary of formal logic, only, to understand and evaluate the reasoning presented in the given arguments.

- The Writing Sample

You will be required to write a simple essay. LSAC does not grade the writing sample, but merely, passes it along to the schools to which you have applied. There are two and only two topic types for the essay. One writing prompt type is *argument*; the other is *decision*. You are allowed 35 minutes to write your essay. No knowledge of the law is required, even though the exercise will generally be some type of argument that you will have to analyze and explain a conclusion. The law schools want to see your skills in reasoning, written communication, organization, writing mechanics, and clarity. It is very important that you write legibly. On the *decision* type prompt you will be required to make a choice between two positions or sides. Both of the sides are good, defensible sides. You are given the facts of the case and you can pick either side to support with your position. There are no right or wrong sides to pick. You will be evaluated on how strongly you can support your position, not which one you picked, and how strongly you can attack the opposing position. A good example: whether or not people should be required under state law to wear seat belts.

The other type of problem that you might be given is *argument*. This type of essay is designed to evaluate your ability to understand and analyze arguments presented on a given topic, and your ability to communicate effectively your evaluation of that argument. The prompt consists of a text in which the author makes a case for some course of action by presenting evidence and claims supported by reasoning. You are required to discuss in detail and evaluate the writer's logic and use of supporting evidence in his argument. This exercise does not ask you to present your personal opinion of the author's argument but rather your evaluation of his conclusions in regard to that topic. You should refrain from letting your personal feeling on a given topic influence your discussion of what is being presented by the author. For instance, you could be evaluating a Supreme Court argument presented on Capital Punishment. Your personal feelings on that topic should never be allowed to enter into the essay you're writing, but should be totally suppressed in favor of the most objective answer you could give on the topic as to the writer's argument, and conclusions. Doing a few of these little test prep exercises before going in to sit for the test should greatly improve your score. Now, we move on to a quick study in law schools to assist you in choosing the right one.

Chapter 5
A Quick Study In Law Schools

From contemplation one may become wise, but knowledge comes only from study.
  -A. Edward Newton   A Magnificent Farce - Chap. 8

As you have already guessed from some of the previous chapters, this book is intended to help potential law school students decide if they really want to be a lawyer and if you are still reading after the last several chapters then you must be fairly dedicated to that idea. So, we can now concentrate on the things that you will need to do to be successful in that endeavor. The people who decide to go into the law are of three types. Those who have either 1)serious financial backing from their relatives, 2) gotten a scholarship, or 3) their financial situation, as it pertains to law school, is less than ideal. This book will emphasize the latter, because that is the situation that most of us find ourselves in when we start to law school. Plus, if you already have the money to attend, you don't need any advice from me on how to afford it. According to the admissions and financial aid offices of the law schools in Alabama - my home state- between 60 and 70 percent of the students that attend obtain some type of financial aid (mostly loans) through their offices. That percentage is even higher when one considers the fact that any student loan that these students obtained from a bank or other financial institution would not be reflected in these numbers. We will discuss student loans and their long lasting effects on lawyers in much more depth in a later chapter.

There are many, many law schools (220 in the U.S.) from which one may pick. But, ironically, none of them will teach you how to be a lawyer. Law school will only teach you *some* law. Furthermore, it won't teach you how to pass the bar exam. You have to take a special review course like BARBRI for that. But, it is still very important to choose one that will suit your individual needs. About 50 percent of the people starting to law school each year are straight out of college. The other half are going to law school as a second thought - either, just got out of the armed forces; decided to make a career change; got tired of having to pay such high legal fees; just now financially able to swing the tuition; or whatever the reason. Many of these have full time jobs and even families. Many of them usually can't afford to quit work and attend law school full time. Going to a school that offers night classes is generally the ticket for these potential students. Any school that doesn't offer night classes is automatically eliminated from consideration for many in this group. Law school curriculums are three years for some schools and some are four years, based on their format. The law school I attended had a four-year curriculum - five nights a week in a semester format, with a fall, spring, and summer semester offered. I would, usually, take a class or two during the summer semester, just so I could have one or two week nights off during the fall and/or spring semester.

-----------------<> ---------------<>------------------

There are many things to consider about the law school you are going to choose. Some of the main considerations are as follows:

1) Reputation

2) Accreditation

3) Cost

4) Financial aid/Scholarship availability

5) Location (how close and what state)

6) Does the school offer a speciality that you are interested in?

7) Day and/or night classes

8) Size of school

9) Size of the classes

10) Social life

11) Physical facilities

We will address each one of these as they relate to the over all objectives that you might have for your law career. Needless to say, where ever you go you will have to be able to balance your priorities to be successful. You will have trade-offs no matter which school you pick. For instance, is it worth the extra tuition and being saddled with huge student loan debt to be able to have a law degree from, say, Harvard Law School? Let me preface this section by saying that I have never had a client or potential client ask me which law school I attended. Some family members, some friends and some persons who were contemplating going to law school have asked me before, but their interest was not to see if I was qualified to represent them but they wanted to know for personal reasons.

1) Reputation

The reputation of the school is important to some potential students and not so important to others. As I previously mentioned, when a potential client walks into a lawyer's office they are not interested in whether he went to Harvard Law or the Holy Mother of Jesus School of Law in Podunk, Kentucky. I have NEVER had a potential client ask me which law school I attended. They just want to know if I can win their case! Can I get them money from the insurance company? Can I keep them out of jail? They are much more interested in <u>their</u> case and its particulars than they are in where I attended law school. They know if I am a licensed attorney that I am "qualified" to take their case. They don't know at that point if I can win their case - I have to convince them of that myself. But generally having a law degree from an Ivy League law school has no importance to the general public when selecting an attorney. We have at least one attorney in our circuit who attended Harvard Law School and from the standpoint of the quality of clients and/or cases that he represents in our circuit, his are generally no better or no worse than any other attorney's cases. He did have a scholarship to attend Harvard, so the financial burden that their tuition presents was, somewhat, mitigated for him. According to a recent *U.S. News & World Report* article, Yale Law School has moved into first place in the ranking of the top ten law schools for 2007 with Stanford Law School coming in second and Harvard Law School falling to third. I don't know just exactly who makes these types of determinations but if it were your desire to graduate from the most prestigious law school in the country, then you would have missed the boat had you started to Harvard two years ago with that as your goal. Simply put, *prestige* can be a fleeting thing.

After you begin to practice and as you are being introduced as the speaker for your monthly local Rotary Club luncheon, then your credentials are going to be mentioned, along with the name of the law school you attended. However, if you won that $19 million verdict in a Ford Pinto accident case recently, then all of the other items on your current resume become merely eye wash. So you see the dilemma facing individuals who don't have plenty of resources available for their law education. I attended law school at Birmingham School of Law,(BSL) and I have never regretted it. Many famous Attorneys and Judges have attended that school. The classes met at night and the tuition was reasonable. I have a friend I'll call Mitch who started to law school the year after I did and he attended Jones Law School in

Montgomery to pursue his J.D. degree. When I finished, I owed $ 0 in student loans. When he finished the next year at Jones, he owed over $ 51,000 in student loans. With everything else being equal, just think about that one fact for a minute. I'm not saying that Jones Law School is better or worse than BSL, but which one of us - Mitch or myself - is going to enjoy the practice of law more. I wouldn't have to take the "loser" cases that he would just to pay the bills. We both passed the bar. We both practice in Alabama. We are both from the same town. We both drive Mercedes. We are about the same age. But he did not enjoy the practice of law and I do. He has now quit practicing and is working for the Social Security Administration. The point is to try to balance getting a "good" law education at the least cost, while factoring in the school's reputation.

2) Accreditation

The accreditation issue is tricky. Some schools are accredited for some things and not for others. What do we mean when we say accreditation? Well, there are law schools that are accredited and law schools that are not, and even different levels of accreditation. For instance, in Alabama there are five law schools, namely, Cumberland Law School, of Samford University, Birmingham; Miles Law School of Miles College, Birmingham; Birmingham School of Law, Birmingham; University of Alabama School of Law, Univ. of Alabama, Tuscaloosa; and Jones Law School of Faulkner University, Montgomery. All of these award the J.D. degree. And if you have a J.D. Degree from any of these and pass the screening by the Bar Membership Committee, then you are allowed to sit for the Alabama Bar Exam. Some people in Alabama apply to law schools that have distance-learning programs such as Kennedy-Western University and others that advertize in the airline (Delta, Southwest, etcetera) in-flight magazines. These programs are taught either on-line or by video tape. They, also, award the J.D. degree for completion of their programs. However, their J.D. degree does not qualify you to sit for the Alabama Bar Exam. None of these programs or schools have been approved (accredited) by the Alabama State Bar Admissions Committee. So, if a person obtains a J.D. from one of these on-line institutions then that person will still not be able to sit for the Alabama State Bar Exam, and hence will not ever be licensed to practice law in Alabama. In other words, they have basically wasted their money and time if they wanted to practice, by choosing the distance-learning approach. You should be certain when making your choice of which law school to attend, that you check with the State Bar Admissions Office in the state in which you intend to practice to be sure that it is approved by them to sit for their Bar Exam. And if you plan to practice in two states, as will be discussed later, then you will need to check with both states on this.

The five in-state law schools that have been approved by the Alabama State Bar mentioned above, have varying degrees of accredation. The Univ. of Alabama Law School and Cumberland Law School are both approved by the *American Bar Association* (ABA). By being ABA approved, these schools graduates have options available to them that graduates of the other three schools don't. It is my understanding that Jones Law School in Montgomery is in the process of seeking accreditation status from the ABA and will probably have obtained that status by the time this book is published. So that would make three of the five that have that status. Both Miles Law School and Birmingham School of Law are not accredited by the ABA. They probably could be if their students pushed it, but in many cases it's just not worth the extra cost.

Being a graduate from one of these ABA accredited schools will allow a person to have a better chance of being accepted into a graduate law program such as the L.L.M. or master of laws program in Taxation or some other such speciality degree. It, also, makes it easier to become licensed to practice in another state. For example, the Tennessee State Bar has a reciprocal agreement with the Alabama State Bar that allows a person who is licensed to practice in Alabama to apply for and obtain a license to practice law in Tennessee without taking the Tennessee Bar Exam, - provided, however, that that

A Survival Guide

person is a graduate of a law school that is ABA accredited. From a personal standpoint that means that I could not become licensed to practice law in Tennessee without having to go back to law school and passing their Bar Exam, since BSL is not ABA accredited. I can still practice in Tennessee on any given individual *case* by applying to their State Bar for *Pro Hoc Vice* status, which allows an attorney from another state to handle *one* case in a jurisdiction in which they are not licensed. So, if you live and intend to practice in an area that is right on the state line, such as, say St. Louis, MO and East St. Louis, IL, then you might want to consider the possibility of becoming licensed to practice in both states. This should be taken into consideration when trying to choose which law school to attend.

3) Cost

This area is probably going to carry the most weight in your decision of which law school to attend. Unless your resources from family or whatever, are pretty much unlimited the cost is going to have to be considered first as to the likelihood of your being able to attend. Most of the people reading this book are not going to fall into the unlimited resources category. If you do you might want to skip this section. Otherwise, read on. The tuition for law school varies widely. Some law schools have tuition costs of less than $4,000 per year while others are well above $35,000. Keep in mind that this does not include text books, room and board, or any other expenses, such as parking permits. The need for some type of financial aid becomes quickly apparent, when all of these factors are considered. One of the least expensive schools that I found on the internet was my law school, BSL, which has tuition costs of about $3,500 per year. The other end of the spectrum revealed that Harvard Law School was one of, if not the most expensive in tuition cost at $37,100 per year. These two are at the extreme ends of the range of law school tuition costs. Jones in Montgomery runs $18,500 per year, while Cumberland at Samford in Birmingham runs just under $25,000. If you plan to be a full time student and live on campus, you are looking at an additional $10-$15 thousand per year. As you can see the cost issue is probably the first issue to be considered during your selection process if you don't have unlimited resources.

Let me give you a little example of just how this plays out, once you begin to practice. I was recently involved with a case where another law firm was associated to help, and one of the attorneys in that firm was a recent BSL graduate (I'll call him Zulu) and one of the other partners was a recent Cumberland graduate (I'll call him Romeo.) I mentioned to them that I graduated from BSL when I saw the BSL diploma on Zulu's wall. He began to brag that he passed the Bar Exam the first time he took it and that Romeo had to take it twice before he passed, even though Romeo had graduated from Cumberland. Then, he added that Romeo still owed over $60,000 in student loans, with a loud laugh. I could see that this had been a very sore spot of contention between these two. And after that little discussion Romeo stayed pissed off for the entire meeting. So, the cost is probably going to carry more weight in your decision than all of these other components combined. The cost factor will impact your practice in many, many ways and for many, many years to come. So, give it the attention it deserves and you will be way ahead of the game when you begin to practice.

4) Financial Aid/Scholarships
- *See Chapter 6 for a full discussion.*

5) Location
The factors to be considered in picking a particular law school based on location are more involved than one might think. Picking a law school in the state in which you are going to practice helps in several ways. First, your tuition is less - no out of state add on. Second, it helps you to be better prepared to take that given state's Bar Exam, as you will be studying that state's law in law school. Third, it helps you to be able to qualify to sit for that state's Bar Exam. But these are only some of the items deserving consideration at this

point. Are you planning to attend as a full-time student or part-time student? Are you planning on keeping your present job or getting another one? Are you going to go during the day or go to night school? Do you want to live at home or on campus? The answers to several of these will usually dictate just where you will have to attend law school, and that is without regard to the school's reputation! If you want to go to Harvard Law and, yet, you want to keep your job as a state trooper, then you have a real dilemma. It should be obvious that these two are mutually exclusive. As previously mentioned, if you will need the income that a job provides then your law school choices will probably be limited. Some law schools do not allow students to work while attending, unless it is in a Clerk capacity for a Judge or some other such closely related part-time position. If you are planning on living at home, continuing to work, and going to law school at night, then you have to choose a school that is close to home. You can't be commuting for four or five hours a day and still maintain all of the other duties that will be required of you. If you are planning to keep your day job and go to night school, then, hopefully, there will be a good school close by that will give you the chance to do just that. On the other hand, if you plan to borrow the money to attend and live on campus then the quality of the legal education you will get will probably be more *fulfilling* than the education of the night student. You will notice that I didn't say *better*, I said more *fulfilling*. The differences between being full time and part time or night student are significant but who's to say which one produces the most well equipped attorney. Going at night and having the responsibility of raising a family at the same time will either galvanize you and make you tough as nails or kill you, - one or the other. Keep in mind that the instructors at these night schools are usually day attorneys and have a lot of practical experience to relate to the student. The other side of that coin is the fact that sometimes these teachers don't know the theory behind why some rules of law are the way they are and if asked a question outside of their area of practice, they may not readily know the answer.

6) Does the school offer a specialty that interests you?

This is generally not a big factor in the selection of a school to attend. Most law schools teach the main core courses and offer only a limited number of electives. If you are interested in tax law or intellectual property or some other specialized legal area, then you might be able to get a course or two in that area as an elective at a law school. However, the proper approach to building a specialized practice is to obtain the law license first. Or in other words, concentrate on passing the bar exam, and then you can specialize. There are many ways one can obtain the courses and/or seminars necessary to build your knowledge in the area that interests you, but this needs to be accomplished *after* you have passed the Bar and begun to practice. There are so many areas of speciality, that it would be impossible for a law school to offer electives in all of them. My law school (BSL) taught the same courses, year after year. That is, everyone who graduated from BSL had taken exactly the same courses as every other student that ever graduated from that school. There were no electives! Everyone took the exact same courses. It is my understanding that their format has changed somewhat since I graduated from there and they now offer a dozen or so electives. We will discuss law school curriculum in more depth in a later chapter.

7) Day or Night classes

This one is of no consequence if you have plenty of financial resources. If you are a full time law student then whether or not you attend classes at night doesn't really make a lot of difference. However, if you are employed full-time then the night school option is probably going to be the only option available to you. So, it doesn't take long to make a decision on this one.

8) Size of School

The size of the school isn't as much of a factor as the ability, from a resources standpoint, to attract well-qualified instructors. If the school is too small it may be unable to afford the well-heeled faculty that some of your larger schools might. Coinciding with this is whether the school is a public or private institution. If the school is a private institution with above average tuition costs then it probably will still be able to afford the type of faculty that one desires for his law education. This might not necessarily be the case for a publicly supported institution that is open to any and all applicants. Tuition costs are a two edged sword. They allow the institution to have great instructors if the cost is expensive. However, if the student lacks the ready resources, the student loan burden after graduation can be a killer.

9) Size of Classes

I have attended law school classes that had six students and law school classes that had 120 students. Both turned out to be good classes for me and I learned a lot from both. Sometimes this issue has more to do with the instructor and his teaching method than with the school environment itself. So this particular issue will generally take care of itself as you become familiar with your law school and the individual instructors for each class.

10) Social Life

This one is easy. If you are attending law school to <u>party</u> then, simply, pick the one that has the best "party school" reputation. Most people go to law school to become attorneys and thereby prepare themselves to have a better chance to party at some later time during their lifetimes but not while in law school. You may want to reevaluate your priorities if partying is a biggie for you.

11) Physical Facilities

If the school has excellent instructors then the facilities become less important. Many times the school, no matter how prestigious, will be undergoing construction or remodeling and classes will be held in a temporary classroom or even a trailer. This will have no bearing on your education if the necessary Internet connections, on-line facilities, and acoustics are adequate.

All of these are fairly important issues to a novice law student. However, as you can see from some of the things just explained, they should be given the level of importance that they deserve. I hope this helps you in your selection process. Now, on to just how we are going to pay for all of this wonderfulness.

Chapter 6

Financial Aid:
How Do I Pay For All Of This Wonderfulness?

A man with a surplus can control circumstances, but a man without a surplus is controlled by them, and often he has no opportunity to exercise judgment.
Harvey S. Firestone

If you're rich, if you have parents who are paying for your law school, or if you have some other source of finances to pay for your law school education, then you can skip this chapter because it examines in detail the financial resource issues associated with attending law school. Many law school students need some sort of financial aid assistance. Keith Norman, executive director of the Alabama State Bar wrote in an article for the May, 2006 *Alabama Lawyer* magazine that of law school graduates in Alabama in 1996, 51 percent of those sitting for the Bar Exam had student loan debt and the average debt amount was $35,000. In 2006, a decade later, those figures had changed respectively to be 35 percent and $71,000. These figures are probably somewhat skewed because any personal loans from banks or other financial institutions that were not associated with the students corresponding law school were not reflected. Classifying the student's debts at the time of the Bar Exam initial sitting as "education debt" resulted in a consistent percentage well above fifty percent over the last ten years.

The article, also, noted that in a recent survey 71 percent of the lawyers in Alabama had agreed that "student loan debt for lawyers practicing for ten years or less, was becoming a significant problem for beginning attorneys." The situation is compounded by the fact that many of these student loans have a variable interest rate, and as prime goes up - and it will soon - these students will have an even larger debt service problem to address at some time in the near future. This study addressed the lawyers in Alabama, only. However, considering the fact that this loan is a <u>federal</u> loan and so easily accessible, this problem is rampant in all other states as well. A person having easy access to a loan of $18,500 per year for three years, ends up with at least $55,500 of student loan debt. If this amount were at a *fixed* interest rate of less than five percent over a ten year period, the payments would still run almost $500 per month. This is part of the reason why the Alabama State Bar has decided to address this, through committee, as an important issue

------------------<>-------------------<>------------------

The types of loans available through the law schools vary, but most schools provide applications for the *Stafford* government loan, which, incidentally, is not credit based. In other words, the application and approval process for this loan is not dependant upon your credit score, so most anyone can qualify. The amount than can be borrowed is up to $18,500 unsubsidized per scholastic year. The only qualification is that you be at least a half time law student, or in other words carry at least what is considered at your law school to be a half load of classes. If twelve hours is considered full time then carrying a load of six semester hours is enough to qualify.

This loan is called the *Federal Direct Unsubsidized Stafford Loan*. As previously mentioned, it is not awarded on the basis of need, but you must apply for federal aid to be considered. The interest on these loans starts to accumulate at the time you receive the money and continues to be charged to the student until such time as the loan is fully repaid. The student may choose to pay the interest while still in school or let it accumulate and be added to the principal. The rate of interest is variable. It gets adjusted every July 1 and is capped at 8.25 percent. The loan carries a 3% origination fee. The repayment begins when the student falls below half-time enrollment or graduates. There is a six month grace period before repayment must begin. The total debt limit for the graduate/professional student = $138,500, if you include the additional subsidized limit.

The easy availability of these loans has contributed tremendously to the number of students deciding to go to law school as full time students. While keeping in mind that this amount will not even cover the cost of tuition at many schools, it is easy to see why many law school students graduate with a debt service level that would choke a horse. This easy access to student loan money is a two edged sword, even though considered a "God send" to many a beginning law school student, it turns into a two headed monster shortly after you graduate. Now consider this, I had previously mentioned that just obtaining the J.D. degree does not allow you to practice - that you must pass the bar exam. Some don't ever pass it. Think about that. A person who has over $100,000 worth of student loan debt finds out that he can't pass the bar! So, he is relegated to paying back this loan while working at his old job as a History teacher at the local high school!

-------------------<>--------------------<>-------------------

Any law students anticipating going the student loan route should follow the following steps to inform themselves as to the possible pit falls associated with doing so:

First. The student should obtain as much information as possible on the types of loans available, along with their associated interest rates. Find out if there is any way that the student can get some of the loan forgiven by working for a state agency or some other such organization after passing the bar.

Second. Research the attorney market in your locale to determine the average starting salary/income for new lawyers for the last couple of years.

Third. Get someone with access to an amortization software program to run an amortization of the moneys that are to be borrowed. This will provide the amount of the monthly payment that will have to be paid each month once you begin to practice until the loan amount is paid off.

Fourth. Use these figures to work up a ratio showing the projected impact that this borrowing will have on your practice and its overall chances of success.

Fifth. Using these figures will allow the individual the chance to understand that this high ratio will in all likelihood preempt that person from jobs like: civil service, public defender, state prosecutor, clerk for Supreme Court Justice, legal services, etcetera. More importantly, these are, generally, jobs that allow the individual to have a regular weekly/monthly paycheck. But because they are lower paying, they are, pretty much, excluded from consideration for anyone who has these huge outstanding student loans, because the debt service to income ratio is too high.

If you can manage to attend law school without borrowing money then you should do so, even if it means attending night classes or attending a law school that doesn't have the big name reputation. The ability to begin your practice completely debt free will help you to enjoy your practice in so many more ways than someone who is burdened with a large student loan debt.

------------------<>--------------------<>-------------------

Another avenue to financing your legal education is to work high paying summer jobs. You say "How do you do that?" Well, there are many jobs out there. You just have to use your imagination. For instance, many oil platforms in the Gulf were damaged during last summer's hurricanes. Underwater welders are at a premium right now. Go to your local YMCA and sign up for their scuba diving classes and become SCUBA certified. This will qualify you for inspector/quality control with one of the big oil companies. Additionally, you could take a couple of welding classes at your local trade school and become qualified to make thousands more during your summer vacation as an underwater welder, etc. Another example - a friend of mine made almost three thousand dollars a month working for an electrical company changing out the blown lights at sports stadiums. This required his climbing poles hundreds of feet tall, but he made almost $ 9,000 in three months and that was years ago when tuition wasn't as expensive. If you're afraid of heights and you can't swim, go to your local bookstore and Noble and buy a twenty dollar *Web Design* book. Spend about three or four months of your spare time learning how to design web sites. Get some business cards printed for thirty dollars and you are now able to charge businesses $2000 per site to set up their web sites. Businesses are clamoring for this service. This is just a few of the ideas that there are for you to think outside the box. There are thousands of things that you can do to earn a very good income for the three months that you have off during the summer. With this money and a little help from relatives you just might be able to complete your law degree with little or no debt.

------------------<>--------------------<>------------------

There are many scholarships, fellowships, assistantships, awards, and grants available for law school study through your chosen law school, as well. Search the internet and see if you can't come up with at least a partial scholarship or grant to help defray your expenses. The company or organization sponsoring this scholarship may require you to major in a subject of their choosing such as *environmental law* or have some other similar stipulation, but you can always add additional courses that you pay for yourself, if you like, as you go along. Some of these may require you to agree to work for the EPA or Legal Services or some other similar organization for two years after you get out. This is a small sacrifice to make to not have any debt coming out of law school. Keep in mind that during those two years that you will be working for them, you will gain some experience, get a regular paycheck, and, in all probability, will be furnished a nice office at no charge. This would allow you to save some of your salary during this time toward furnishing and establishing your own private office for practice when this period is completed. These are just some of the options available to potential law school students to assist in defraying the staggering cost of law school attendance. Be tenacious. Be aggressive. And above all, be thorough, in your search for financial assistance.

Once you have passed the LSAT, chosen which law school to attend, and decided how you will pay for your law education, the next step is to mentally prepare yourself for what you can expect in law school. Law school has it's own culture and can eat you alive if you aren't, at least somewhat, prepared for what awaits you when you get there. The next chapter attempts to give you a little insight into the law school culture.

Chapter 7

LAW SCHOOL: What to expect.

The roots of education are bitter, but the fruit is sweet.
Aristotle

Law school has its own culture, and it will take you quite a while, at best, to adjust to it. It is so different from college that some students are never able to accept it for what it is and they just drop out. The teachers help to perpetuate this culture at first, because all the students know that the instructors are lawyers and the students have that *mystique* about their *lawyer* teachers. Not only are they lawyers, they can, also, give you an "F." I went to law school at Birmingham School of Law (BSL), which had night classes five nights a week. I would leave work every day at 5:00 p.m. and drive 60 miles to school. The classes started at 6:30 p.m. and were over at 8:30 p.m. I would, then, drive the 60 miles back home and get home at about 10:00 p.m. That routine got *old* fast. But I had a friend (I'll call him, Robert) who, also, was attending and so we began to ride together. That helped us to encourage each other to not skip classes. This friend and I had both graduated from Jacksonville State University with a BS degree in Math and we were both ill prepared for the culture shock we received in law school.

One of the first things that you will need to learn about law school is to have the proper approach or to put it another way - proper point of view. Based on which law school you attend, you may have teachers who practice law during the day and teach law school classes at night, or teachers who have never practiced law and only have an ivory tower, i.e., theoretical, knowledge of the law. Or you could have a combination of these two. Some schools such as Cumberland School of Law in Birmingham have some teachers who have never practiced law. Never won a case. Never tried a case. And never been inside a courtroom unless they were there to pay a traffic ticket! Some law schools even have instructors who have never taken the Bar Exam. But, if your career goal is to become a legal *scholar* and become a law school professor then a law school with this type of faculty might be best suited for you. However, if your intent is to become a lawyer and practice law then you might have more interest in a school that has instructors that are practicing lawyers. The BSL faculty was 100 percent attorneys in active practice or who had just retired from the active practice of law. In my opinion this allowed us, the students at BSL, to have a more realistic understanding of the practice of law. The instructors were always able to provide real life examples of cases that they had handled that exemplified the rule of law or legal theory that was being studied in that class. On the other hand, some of the text books that we were using in those classes were written by these very same *ivory tower* types that I was just trashing above.

So, in order to have the proper perspective, you have to see the over all, big picture and understand where you will be fitting into that picture. Some of the instructors that I had were multi-millionaires. And it was not at all uncommon for a teacher to come into class smiling and boasting about just settling or winning a million-dollar case. Although I didn't always know exactly how to take the boasting, it still reinforced my notion that I was doing the right thing by going to law school. So in that way, it was always good when one of the teachers did this. Several of the teachers were cocky, but almost all were fair. No matter which law school you choose, you will have some instructors that you really like and some that you can't stand, but most will be good, honest, and fair. That was the case at BSL, and it will be with your school, too. At BSL I had four teachers over the course of the four years that I could not stand. They were egotistical. They were not good teachers and they thought they were great teachers. They flunked everybody they could. One of them even counted off five points for each word you misspelled on his final. They thought that it was their job to weed out all the students that they didn't like, and none of the four liked me, because I always said what I thought. My disdain for all of them grew to the point that I took the four courses that they taught at another law school across town and transferred the credits back to BSL, just so I wouldn't have to put up with their attitudes. But most of your teachers will be fair. Most of mine approached their jobs as teachers with the right perspective. They taught the students as best they could and graded everyone based upon their performance on the exams. More importantly, they knew that the Bar Exam would weed out any and all slackers and that it was not necessary for them to flunk half the class just to make a point.

-------------------<>-------------------<>-------------------

The teaching method most commonly used in law school is the *case* method. That is, real life cases are studied and the student is required to read, understand, and brief (i.e., prepare a summary of) these cases for class. Some law school professors refer to this as the *Socratic* method, so named after the ancient Greek philosopher Socrates. Socrates employed a method of teaching by which he more or less required his students to study and reason their way through the problems that he presented to them. In a way, he let them teach themselves, while he acted mainly as their coach. This is a good approach to teaching the law because it forces the student to see both sides of an issue. Many of our texts had cases on a certain point of law that would defend one side of an issue and then, immediately, present another case with the exact same facts that defended the other side of that same issue. One could readily see that many of these cases which had very, very similar fact situations in both cases were decided very differently in Court. The Plaintiff (i.e., person doing the suing) would win the case in, say, North Carolina, while almost the exact same fact situation in another later case in, say, Ohio might result in a verdict for the Defendant (i.e., the person being sued). So, one of the most difficult concepts for a new law school student to grasp is that there is not ever an exact right answer in a civil case. These always must be decided on a case by individual case basis.

With my background in Math and Accounting, the principle that there might be more than one RIGHT answer to a given problem/case was very difficult for me to grasp. I was probably in my third year before I was really comfortable with that concept. Now, if a case involved a matter relating to a law that was already on the books, then it was not a problem because that law would dictate the outcome. Let's say, for instance, that someone waited too long to return a new car that was a *lemon* to the dealer where he bought it. Well, the lemon law puts a specific deadline on that issue and the customer has to abide by it or he loses. However, most lawsuits involve unique situations - a backyard property line dispute, for instance - that don't have specific laws that have been passed to cover them, therefore, the *need* for each case being decided on a case by case basis. If there were always an easy, obvious, RIGHT answer, we wouldn't need lawyers or juries. The jury decides what the *right* answer is. Whether the jury's answer is the *right* answer is, itself, sometimes, questionable because the jury might be split 7-5 in favor of one side or the other. So, seven decided that side one is right, and five decided that side two was right. Furthermore, many times the case is appealed and a different outcome results from the Appeals Court, or they order a new trial, which could in turn have a completely different jury and, more importantly, outcome.

The cases that we studied in law school, where, given a common set of facts, the plaintiff won in one case and the defendant won in another case eventually made me think that the outcome was probably different because of the *effect* that the attorney for each side had on the case. I remember one fact situation in particular that really drove this point home. It was from two cases we had in Torts class - one from Georgia and one from Virginia. They were from the 1930's and the facts went something like this:

Mr. Plaintiff had a hound dog and it kept going in Mr. Defendant's yard and killing his chickens. Back then everybody had chickens. Defendant told Plaintiff that he was tired of it and the next time it happened that he was going to shoot the dog. Well, it happened again and Defendant shot Plaintiff's dog and killed it. Well, a Georgia jury awarded Mr. Plaintiff a sum of money for his dead hound. Whereas, in the Virginia case, a Virginia jury, with exactly the same set of facts, awarded Mr. Defendant a sum of money for his dead chickens. Go figure.

------------------<>--------------------<>------------------

The case method is very effective. It causes the student to have to examine all sides of an issue, but its main strength is that it makes the student have to *think*. An exemplar of why this teaching method is so effective can easily be found in the course work for Constitutional Law. The Constitutional Law class lasts two semesters. The *U.S. Constitution* itself, including the amendments, is not but eighteen pages long but yet the text that we used in my Constitutional Law class was about 900 pages. There were hundreds of cases, maybe even in excess of a thousand cases, covered in the book. There were cases on:

. The Legislature and its structure (redistricting, etc.)
. The Executive Powers of the President
. Eminent domain

- Enforcement of Treaties
- Power of the States
- Supremacy
- Religion
- Free speech
- Assembly
- Petition
- Press
- Militia
- Right to bear arms
- Quartering of Soldiers
- Searches

- Seizures
- Grand Juries
- Double Jeopardy
- Self-Incrimination
- Due Process
- Equal Protection
- Miranda warnings
- Common Law trial by Jury
- Bail
- Cruel & unusual punishment
- Slavery
- Citizenship
- States rights
- Prohibition & its repeal
- Voting rights
- Income taxes

The list could go on and on, but the point is that any and all viewpoints on these issues were studied in detail. An appreciation and understanding of the Constitution and the ways in which different lawyers, individuals, and judges had read and interpreted its meaning was gained by all who were in the class, including myself. Much would have been lost and left unexplored in its interpretation if the text had only explained the meaning of each article or amendment on its face. A text written using that approach would probably not have been more than 100 pages long. One could say that a text of that nature, once read and memorized, would give one an understanding of the Constitution, but I think you can readily see that the *case* method approach that was used was much more effective and educational to us.

------------------<>-------------------<>------------------

For the first two years of law school, most of your teachers will require you to read cases and write a *brief* (summarization) about each of those cases. Incidentally, the first thing you should do when you start to law school is go to the book store and buy a Law Dictionary. This is a must. As you read your texts and brief your cases, especially for the first year or so, you will constantly come across words that you don't know. Even if you have heard of them previously, you still won't know their definition. So, having a Law Dictionary is a must! This ability to quickly learn what a legal term means will do wonders for your self confidence, and will help make you feel more like you belong. I even bought myself a *pocket* law dictionary and kept it in my briefcase, so I could look up words when no one was looking. You might be assigned as many as 100 cases per week. At my law school we would average about twenty per class or, roughly, 100 per week. And we usually didn't have to turn them in. We just had to have them ready in case the teacher called on us to "brief" the case in class. Most of the classes consisted of the teacher choosing a case and then picking a student to stand up and "brief" it to the class. If he called on you and you didn't have it, you would get a zero for that class, not to mention being embarrassed in front of your classmates. But, that much reading and "briefing" made for an extremely long weekend, which was the only time I had to catch up since I had class five nights a week. I think that, collectively, the law schools assign this enormous amount of reading during this first year as a part of the weeding out process. Those that aren't serious, but are just going to law school because Daddy wanted them to, usually don't make it through this period. So, after about two months of this "briefing" homework and seeing that if something didn't change, that my wife was going to leave me, I decided to find a way around so much reading. Something had to give. Back at school, we formed a work group. I assembled five other guys and we assigned each person three or four cases that each was to brief for each class, each week. Then the night of that class we would meet in the hall and exchange photocopies of these briefed cases with each other. This worked well and none of us ever got a zero after that.

------------------<>-------------------<>------------------

While the discussion of the different class subjects (curriculum) that you will take in law school is covered in another chapter, you should know that the types of assignments given will vary from teacher to teacher and class to class. And, fortunately, not all classes call for the briefing of cases. You will have legal research which requires you to go to the law library and look up stuff. Moot Court will require you to actually attempt to *try* a case against your classmates. Some teachers, based on which course they're teaching, may require you to write a "research paper." While other teachers will only require you to attend class, listen to the lectures, and to take the exam(s). Most classes have only *one* exam, with that being the final. This presents another major adjustment problem for the new law school student. Everyone is used to having several exams per semester during their undergraduate course work and not having but one exam per course per semester is just too much pressure. Many students drop out during the first semester because some of the legal terminology is very confusing and intimidating. (Yo, where's their law dictionary?) Also, they haven't had any exams or grading feedback at that point, so they don't know where they stand. But keep in mind that no one else does, either. That first four months - the first semester- is difficult because you really don't know how you're doing. My friend, Robert, had an extremely hard time during this period and it was difficult for me to convince him to not drop out. He felt that he was "lost" and wouldn't ever be able to catch up. I, finally, convinced Robert that if he would just wait another three to four weeks, the finals would be over and he could always drop out then if he had flunked his finals. Luckily, he made all A's and B's. This reassured him and things went much better after that. But the first semester usually has about a 10-15% drop out rate, because of some of the factors just mentioned.

 Over the course of your three to four years there, the culture becomes more apparent as you become more in tune with your classmates and their reasons for being there. All of the different motivations that each of them had for deciding to go to law school will come out. It will present itself in their arguments, in the elective courses that they choose to take, and in the conversations that you have with them at the campus coffee shop. Some of them will say they are there, not to pass the Bar and practice, but that they merely wanted to learn the Law. Some of my classmates said that. But in the final analysis, most all will wind up taking the Bar Exam just, if for no other reason, to see if they can pass it. When I started to law school, I didn't know if I wanted to practice or not. I mainly was going to learn the Law since I had to work with various and sundry types of contracts in my computer business. Sometimes, I had to write a computer maintenance contract myself because none of the lawyers in town at that time knew a *bit* from a *byte*. So, I would, basically, be writing my own contracts and having my attorney proofread them and then bill me $500.00. That, along with some encouragement from my wife was why I went to law school. But the closer you get to graduation, the more you think that maybe you should take the Bar Exam since its just takes three days and only has a $200 application fee.

--------------------<>--------------------<>--------------------

Getting back to the classes themselves, don't get behind in your cases - whether reading, briefing, or whatever assignment you're given. If you have a job, and you ever get behind, it is almost, if not, impossible to catch up. Eventually, you will be forced to just withdraw because you will feel like you're drowning if you don't stay caught up with the rest of the class. New assignments come with every class and if you put them off you will not have the time to do all of them before they are due. I spent every weekend trying to catch up that week's assignments. Robert and I would try to split the work whenever we could, but it still was very difficult to stay caught up with the level of work that we were assigned. He did not have a job, so he was able to keep his homework more up to date than I could. Obviously, it is much easier for someone to attend law school full time than to work and go to law school, too. I would strongly recommend that you attend as a full time student if there is any way possible that you can afford to do so. Your stress level will be much, much more manageable.

Adding to the culture is the competition between students. And the competition can be quite fierce at times. There will be times that an instructor will assign the class a case to look up and/or brief that is not covered in your text book. And one of the first students to get to that reference book in the law library will take the book, look up the case, brief the case and then put the book back in the wrong place on the wrong shelf, thereby hiding it from the other students. Some students would even go as far as to tear out the pages for that case, so that no one else could see it. This is not as much of a problem now that the Internet provides most of the research tools for these cases, but at the time I was there, this would happen all the time. So, that person would make an "A" and everyone else would make a zero!

Another tip that can help is to find students who had your particular instructors the year before and see if you can get copies of any of their old tests. Most of the instructors are too lazy to make up a complete new test each semester, so any old tests that you can find to use as a guide will be very valuable to you in your studies for the finals. Some of my instructors encouraged us to try and locate some of their old finals, especially during the first and second semesters, so we would have a better understanding of what to expect on the finals. With the final usually being the only factor determining your grade, it was very important to see beforehand what kind of test the instructor gave. During my first and second year, I would take that particular instructor's last two or three old tests and look up the answers to all the questions, and memorize the answers before I went in to take that final. Many times, 70 to 80% of the test would be questions that I already had memorized! This is a BIG help, especially during the first and second semesters, when you don't have a clue what to expect.

What to expect in law school, also, has to address the courses themselves. I do that in summary form in the up coming chapter.

Chapter 8
Law School Curriculum & The Real World

Thunder is good, thunder is impressive; but it is the lightning that does the work.
Mark Twain - Letter to an unidentified person.

In trying to decide what to include in this book, many things were considered. Understandably, since the main theme of this treatise is an attempt to assist individuals who think they might like the law as a profession, I decided to include a chapter on just what general areas are covered in law school, i.e. the law school curriculum. Not only do most of the individuals choosing to go into the law know very little about what lawyers do, they know even less about what law schools teach. We've already discussed law school culture to some degree, but not much about law school subject matter. As I go through this I will try to point out just why each subject is studied and what, if any, degree of importance it has in the overall big picture of the Law. Maybe this will help you be able to have a general understanding of what is going to be facing you in the law school classroom when you get there.

To help set the tone for this discussion, consider this: in law school I had one course in criminal law and one course in criminal procedure.

That's *two* classes out of the total of 44 that I took. That works out to 5 percent of my law school classes. And yet there are more than twice as many criminal cases filed in court as civil cases in the real world. "So, why doesn't the law school curriculum more accurately reflect the real world in actual case volume?" you might ask. Well, some subjects you may take, such as Estate Tax, you will probably never see again, unless it's on the Bar Exam. While others, such as Civil Procedure, you will use on a daily basis. Looking at it another way may help us to understand the level of importance assigned to certain areas/courses and how they impact daily practice.

The *Code of Alabama* is the volume of books that contains all of the laws applicable in the Alabama State Courts. These laws were passed by the Alabama Legislature. Recall from one of the earlier chapters that law falls into two categories - case law (common law) and statutory law (Code of Al.). Statutory law is the codified law or written law, and tells us directly what are the elements of a crime. Whereas, the case or common law addresses cases that have no written code, only prior similar cases that have been decided by Courts to go by. These include such things as property line disputes, etcetera.

The law is vast and extensive. There are many different areas or specialties in the law. These range from pro basketball agents to bank trust department lawyers to social security disability attorneys and everything in between. It would be impossible for a law school to offer courses in all of the different areas that the law covers. There are just too many. And many times during your classroom time in law school you may wonder to yourself if you will ever actually *use* the subject being taught. I know I did. There are some courses such as "Insurance," for instance, that you may never need or see again in your lifetime. And Insurance is not covered on the Bar Exam. So, why was it required? That's a good question. The Law Schools try to offer courses that are as current as possible with the legal environment in the state and still maintain the "core courses" that are tested on the Bar Exam. Some of the classes I was required to take in law school, I have never used. Not on the Bar Exam, and certainly not in practice. But those classes are very few. The yearning of lawyers to be well versed and educated in as many of the varying areas of the law as possible, produces a better lawyer. So just accept it for what it is and don't complain if a course or two appears on your class schedule that you think are a waste of time.

------------------<>--------------------<>------------------

In this section, I will just cover a list of the "main" subjects and a simple explanation of what each is. (For a complete list of law school courses covered in law school see appendix A.)

. Torts
. Contracts: including UCC.
. Equity
. Domestic Relations
. Real Property
. Criminal Law
. Procedure - Civil & Criminal
. Wills & Trusts
. Business Entities
. Tax
. Conflicts of Law

------------------<>--------------------<>------------------

Torts:
Until I started to law school I had never heard of the word "Tort." I had been involved in several law suits, both as plaintiff and defendant. However, that term was never used. A "tort" is defined by the law dictionary as "a civil wrong, giving rise to a cause of action, independent of contract." It is covered in two semester courses. It

details what, how, when and where torts occur and their remedies. The usual remedy for a tort against a person or their property is *money* damages, - not always but usually. If you're walking through your local hardware store and a sales associate drops a bag of top soil on your head, you have been "*torted.*" Keep in mind that this person probably didn't intend to do this, and feels terrible about it happening. But, torts don't have to be intentional. If you get out of your car at your neighbor's house and go inside to play bridge, only to hear a crash, look outside and see your car crushed up against another car across the street because you forgot to put your car in park, then the person whose car was crushed has been *torted*. You may hate it worse than he does, because now your insurance goes up, you won't have a car to drive while it's being fixed, and the repair costs on your Mercedes are always terribly expensive.

If someone punches you in the nose for making fun of the *Auburn Tigers*, then that is battery and a crime punishable by time in jail and a fine. Just as importantly, it is, also, a tort. You can sue that person when he gets out of jail for the damages to your person, and clothes. In this case, the tort *was* intentional. So, there are two kinds of torts, intentional and unintentional (negligence.) If you told your landlord at your apartment complex three weeks ago that two of the steps on the stairway leading to your apartment were rotted from the rain and he doesn't get them fixed and someone falls because of the step giving way, then the landlord has committed the tort of negligence, and the injured party may recover money damages.

It is important to understand that not every event that injures a person is a tort. For instance, let's say that you are going to the grocery store to pick up some bananas and milk while heading home after work. It comes a strong thunderstorm just as you get out of your car to enter the store. Right next to the entrance everyone has deposited the water from the tops of their umbrellas just as they came inside. The floor there is extremely wet although the rain shower is only about a minute old. You slip in the water and fall, breaking your arm. Just as you sit up from the fall, you see the store assistant manager approaching the front of the store with a large yellow cone that says "Caution- Wet Floor." This scene would make you think that you had been "torted" since you now have a broken arm and the management knew that the floor was wet and slippery. Right? Well, not so fast, my friend. The store didn't make the rain. God did. And the store was trying to warn the customers that the floor was wet, which is their only responsibility. So, this is an *accident*. Your chances of monetary recovery under these circumstances would be slim to none. If you are the one sitting there in pain, it may not seem fair. However, if you are the owner of the store and knew that every time it rained, you stood the chance of being sued and losing, then we wouldn't have any grocery stores, and would all have to grow our own food!

Notice that the definition given above for tort excluded contracts, I will now address that area of the curriculum.

Contracts:

This is a freshman course and covers two semesters. The concept of a legal contract is simple really: two or more people form an agreement on some action to be taken that will benefit both (all) parties involved. The first part of the course covers the elements of a contract, who can be a legal party to a contract, and things such as how long a contract lasts. The second part of the course covers deeper theory, such as, when an "oral" contract is valid, the enforceability and nature of "implied contracts," and contracts that are covered by the U.C.C. (Uniform Commercial Code)

Criminal:

This is a one semester course and is usually taught in the second year. This course is easy. Everything that is a crime in Alabama, is listed in the *Alabama Code*. That is - everything that is classified by the State as a crime. Some things, like IRS income tax evasion, are Federal crimes and can be committed in Alabama but they are not punishable or enforceable by the State. Anyone who would like to know what constitutes a particular crime, such as, say burglary, can go on the internet to the State's website and look in the Code. The necessary elements of the crime are listed, along with the associated punishment if convicted.

Business Entities:

This area is actually several courses: corporations, agency and partnerships, LLC, etcetera. The types of organizations or entities under which business is done in the state are explored in detail. Legally, business is defined as any activity performed with the intent to make money or income.

Sole Proprietor:

If this activity is done by one person, such as say, "John Doe's Lawn Care Service" then it is called a <u>sole proprietorship</u>. This means that one person gets all the money from cutting the grass. He is responsible for the business, and, also, responsible for paying all of the expenses for the business, including the taxes. He is, also, liable for any torts or problems that happen during the course of doing business. He may even hire several employees to help him. He may even hire thousands of employees to help him if he gets the contract to keep the state's interstate highway right of way mowed. And no matter how many employees he has, he is still the one responsible and liable for the business. Although, this is the most risky and usually least profitable way to do business, it is the most common. There are more sole proprietary type businesses in the U.S. than all of the other business types combined. Every neighborhood flower shop, barber shop, auto repair, or lawn service is usually a sole proprietorship.

Partnership:

This type of Business entity is defined as two or more individuals coming together to do business as partners. Basically we have two sole proprietors who decide that two heads are better than one. Many times in a partnership, one partner will provide the business expertise and the other partner will provide the financing for the business. These partners are responsible for the business. They get all the money. They are responsible for all of the expenses, including the taxes. Generally, unless there is an agreement to the contrary, they both share everything 50-50. They are jointly and severally responsible for all of the business' liabilities. These type businesses are like sole proprietorships with regard to liability and being sued. In other words, there is no protection.

Examining all of the advantages and disadvantages of each business entity type would be <u>way</u> beyond the scope of this book and could probably be a book in and of itself. However, I would like to mention before I leave the discussion of <u>sole proprietorships</u> that a business operating as such is at great risk by doing so and give you an example of what that means. For argument's sake, let's say that one of John's employees is cutting the grass at a Doctor's house up on the mountain, and the Doctor's kids, ages 14,10, and 4 are swimming in the backyard pool. Let's, also, say that the brakes on the mower are worn out but John has not had time to get them replaced because he's been so busy. So, he told the employee to just drive *slow*. The four year old gets out of the pool, steps on the wet grass and slides down the incline toward the mower. The employee sees her but can't stop in time and her left foot is mangled by the blade. The next day John finds out that the wound was so severe that her foot had to be amputated! Now, the employee didn't run over her foot on purpose. But there is still enough liability with this scenario that, even if John has insurance, he is in trouble. Instead of making money cutting grass, he is probably going to lose his house, his car, and a good percent of any money he might earn in the future.

This fictitious injury should give you a fairly good understanding of why it is important for a person in business to try to limit his/her personal liability as much as possible as it relates to the business' activities. And although it is not possible to avoid all of the risk associated with operating a business, it is possible, if approached properly, to greatly limit your *personal* exposure to monetary liability damages. The most obvious way to limit your liability is to have good liability insurance. Beyond that, the smartest way to limit your liability is to set the business up as the type of business entity that affords limited liability to the owners by state statute.

In layman's terms, that means the people starting a business need to set the company up as a Corporation or Limited Liability Company.(LLC) The state rules for setting up these types of business entities vary from state to state. But generally speaking, all states have established by state statute the right for these two distinct types of business entities to be formed and the right to become licensed and conduct business in their respective states. Doing this usually takes the business owners (save some extreme special circumstances) out of the picture as to business liability in the day-to-day operation of the business. This is not to say that this protection is 100 %, because the owner of a Corporation could take the company tow motor and run over his wife's boyfriend. *That* owner would still have liability. However, the shareholders/owners of a Corporation and members of an LLC are usually limited to no damages personally. Usually, only the LLC or corporation is liable for any business related damages.

Corporations:

Almost all of the *major* businesses in the U.S. are this type of business entity. All states have passed statutes authorizing the establishment of corporations by their Secretary of State. Corporations have several advantages over sole proprietorship and partnerships. Corporations exist through the issuance of shares. Sometimes referred to as stock, these "shares" afford the corporation the ability to raise capital for the initial set up or expansion of the business. This stock is what you see that is bought and sold on the New York stock exchange and the NASDAQ. Most corporations are too small to be viably listed on the major stock exchanges and are generally held or owned by family, friends, company employees and the like. These are called closely held corporations. The larger corporations such as Exxon, Ford, etcetera have followed the required regulations to have their stock publicly traded on one of the major exchanges. Another advantage to doing business as a corporation is that the owners have limited liability. Except under very, very unusual circumstances the owner's liability for the corporation's business related activities is limited to the amount of his/her capital investment in the corporation and that usually came from the purchase of the stock. Corporations are, also, taxable entities unto themselves and have to file annual tax returns in somewhat the same fashion as individuals do, except that the IRS forms and schedules are different for corporations.

LLC:

Another form of business entity is fairly new, having only come about in the last twenty years or so. It is called the Limited Liability Company. (LLC) These were established by the individual State Legislatures, and most states now have this type of business entity. LLCs don't have "stock" like a corporation, but it's owners are called "members." This type of business entity has liability protection for it's members, as well. The members are not liable for business related torts or activities except in very unusual circumstances. This form of business entity is less formal and easier to set up than a corporation and has become very popular lately. It is preferred as the entity of choice over partnerships, primarily because of the liability protection.

Domestic Relations:

This course covers divorce, child custody, adoptions, and more. It tackles such topics as the legal grounds that are available to a person in that state for obtaining a divorce - adultery, insanity, incompatibility and about ten others. Also, covered are such things as the elements that constitute a "common law" marriage; the different types of adoption; when a spouse is entitled to alimony in a divorce and how much; how custody in divorce actions work, etcetera.

Real Property:

Most law schools have two to three courses in Real Property. The topics covered range from deeds to property line disputes to statutory rights and remedies in land. These courses will usually have a peripheral coverage of mortgages as they relate to property transactions. Additionally, you are expected to learn how land is formatted in sections for the purposes of deed legal description text: Township, Range, NW quarter of the SE quarter, and so forth. This is difficult, even for someone like me who had a good bit of geometry in college. Complicating the real property picture was the fact that two of the teachers that taught the real estate courses at BSL were S.O.B.s who felt like the job of a good teacher was to fail as many students as possible, scare the Hell out of everyone in class and then smoke cigarettes and tell jokes for the rest of that class meeting. Even if the subject matter had been less difficult, I'm sure that I would still have developed an aversion to Real Property. I've done a few property deeds and I've done a few mortgages in my practice (sometimes you have no choice) but it's not on my shingle.

Wills and Trusts:

This is usually taught in two courses covering Wills, Trusts, and Estates. Even though this doesn't sound like it would be a big money producing area for a law practice, it is covered heavily on the Bar Exam and is very important to know. Many times a lawyer will be asked by a client to prepare a will, and that will open the door for the lawyer to perform many other more important tasks for that client. You may not charge but $150.00 to do the will, but that doesn't reflect any repeat business that that client might give you. The bar exam covers this area heavily, because the state bar wants to insure that no one *ever* becomes a lawyer in that state that doesn't, at the very least, know how to prepare a valid will.

Equity:

This course covers two semesters. It is an important course and is also covered heavily on the Bar Exam. Sometimes there are situations in business and even someone's personal life where a "tort" has occurred and money damages just won't do! That's where a court of equity comes in. An example of this would help. Let's suppose for argument's sake that after you become an attorney you accidentally hire a nympho to be your secretary and after about two weeks on the job you realize from the comments that she has been making and the low cut dresses that she has been wearing that it's not just a pay check she is interested in from you. Further, let's say that you fire her rather than jeopardize your marriage. She gets extremely upset and tells you that she has *never* been rejected before and that you will be sorry. The next Monday you arrive at your office, only to be greeted on the front sidewalk by this lady in a bikini carrying a sign saying what a scum-bag lawyer/employer you are. And since it is on a public city sidewalk next to the main street through town she is not trespassing. You wouldn't have to be a rocket scientist to know that this might hurt your practice. But just how do you go about getting this person to stop! Well, you can petition a Court of Equity to Order this person to cease and desist this type of activity. If the Judge hears her argument and your argument and decides that you did nothing wrong, he should order her to stop this picketing. If she continues to picket after this Equity Order has been served on her then she can be arrested and put in jail for contempt of Court. There are other instances that occur, many times in business settings, where this type of Order/Action is necessary to stop someone from doing something that harms another business. Any time you need someone to legally perform a particular action or to stop performing a particular action and you nor your attorney can convince them to do so, equity court is, many times, the last and only resort available to you. These orders are called injunctions or restraining orders. They can be either temporary or permanent in disposition, and they can order performance or the halt of a performance. These are civil cases and the Equity Court is a civil court. However, the threat of jail time for Contempt of Court, almost makes their function seem similar to a criminal court that can send someone to jail.

Procedure - Civil & Criminal:

This one is split between civil and criminal because the filing procedures differ between the two. The civil procedure course lasts two semesters, while the criminal procedure course lasts one semester. There are very stringent rules that are set up by the State and Federal Courts that have to be followed when dealing with those Courts from a procedure standpoint. You have certain distinct time limits on some things - called "statute of limitations." Various other deadlines apply as well, depending upon the type of case you are dealing with. For example the statute of limitations on, say, an automobile accident is two years from the time of the accident. What the state legislature decided on these types of torts is that if you are involved in an accident and the other driver has "torted" you -i.e. it was his fault- you should be able to determine just how bad and how much he has torted you and bring your cause of action against him within a two year period after the wreck. This is a reasonable time and puts all parties on notice that the period to file is two years. If you get lazy and don't file within that time then you are forever barred from bringing an action against that person for those damages. The law makers felt that this was long enough. After five years, people die, people forget, people move to other states, and things change to the point that the case would not be nearly as judicious as it would if brought in a timely manner. The procedures, also, are specific in listing the format for filings - complaints, answers, motions and the like. The guidelines, also, cover appeals to higher courts including the time limits and formats. Many of these procedure rules are now propagated on electronic filing. Many of the Courts that attorneys presently have to use have mandatory requirements for electronic filing. If you don't have someone knowledgeable about computer filings in your law office then you are going to have many problems with the Courts and Judges. Keep in mind that the procedure must be followed to the letter, and you can have the law, the facts, and the witnesses on your side in a big case and still lose it because of the technicality of not following the proper procedure. So, you need to pay close attention in these classes. I ordered a copy of the Alabama procedure rules that is published every year by West Law as a reference book to use during this course. This turned out to be a big advantage for me because it was indexed and I could look up anything being covered in class and find out what the rule was in Alabama almost immediately as it was being covered in class.

Conflicts of Law:

This is a one semester course and covers the jurisdictional issues that sometimes arise in cases. By jurisdictional rules, I mean which Court has the Constitutional Right to try the instant case. For instance, let's say that I am on vacation with my family going out West to see the Grand Canyon. Further, let's say that I have an auto accident in Dallas, TX. The driver of the car that hits my car is on vacation as well and he lives in Detroit, MI. This is strictly a civil action unless he was intentionally trying to run me over. His insurance company is in Indiana, while my Insurance company is in Illinois. The policeman that wrote the accident report is a Dallas city cop. First, the other driver doesn't want the case tried in Alabama because the Alabama judge might be in my Sunday School Class. I don't want the case tried in Michigan because I just don't trust *"Yankees."* I'm sure his insurance company would prefer the case be tried in Indiana where their Corporate attorneys could handle the case without them having to hire local counsel if it's tried elsewhere. However, it makes judicial economic sense for the case to be tried in Dallas, TX where the accident occurred, for several reasons. Any possible witnesses are there. The cop is located there. The local traffic rules apply. The jury may make a request to view the accident scene and/or for other reasons. Generally, jurisdiction vests in the Court where the accident/crime/event that precipitated the case happened. In this case that is Dallas, TX. There is an additional requirement linked to the amount of the money damages being demanded. Small Claims Court jurisdiction, or some other Court's jurisdiction may apply sometimes based upon the dollar amount.

These kinds of conflicting scenarios happen all the time since we are such a mobile society and just about everybody has a car. So, just where is the proper place to hold a trial? In some jurisdictions/Circuits, the County/Circuit is so small that the jury pool is made up of *relatives* of each other. Everyone is, in some way, kin to everyone else. In other words, the family tree in that County doesn't fork much. Getting a fair jury of one's peers in that County might be extremely difficult. The defense attorney in some cases will ask for the trial to be moved to another venue or Circuit because of the negative publicity that his client has received about the case. And many times, the Judge will grant that Motion, because the Judge knows that it will be extremely difficult to find 12 people out of the jury pool that have not been exposed to details of the facts in the case and who have, subsequently, already drawn an opinion as to that person's guilt.

------------------<>--------------------<>------------------

Other circumstances sometimes apply. If two drug addicts rush into a branch office of a local bank in downtown Birmingham, and rob the teller using a pistol. When they are apprehended, they will probably not be tried in the Circuit Court of Jefferson County, AL. They will probably be tried in the Federal Court of the Northern District of Alabama by the federal prosecutors, because the bank is insured through FDIC, and thereby the robbery falls under the jurisdiction of the Federal Government. A state crime has been committed as well and the perpetrators could be tried in Federal Court and, later, in State Court as well. But that usually doesn't happen. Same result if someone robs a U.S. Postal worker. So, the jurisdictional issue is complicated at times. A Birmingham City cop can give someone a speeding ticket in Birmingham, AL but, if he is transporting a prisoner to Gulfport, MS and encounters a speeder in that city, then he just ignores it or possibly radios it in. However, he is out of his jurisdiction and has no authority to give a ticket at that location. Logically, this is the way it should be because he may be familiar with the 35 mph speed limit in Birmingham and it could be 45 mph in Gulfport, and him not know it. Whereas, a Gulfport cop would be familiar with that fact.

Tax:

This covers Individual and Corporate Income Tax during the first semester of the senior year, and then Estate and Gift Tax during the second semester of your senior year. I was already fairly familiar with the individual and corporate tax rules due to the fact that I did my personal tax returns and my Corporate tax return for my computer business. I, also, had experienced many tax related interactions with the trucking and hardware store clients that BSI had support contracts with. Their CPA's would occasionally have a question and since I was the one who designed and wrote our General Ledger Package, I was the one to answer any questions they might have. The course included exercises in both individual and corporate tax returns. And it wouldn't hurt to take a seminar or some similar accounting refresher course before tackling these two courses.

-------------------<>--------------------<>-------------------

This is, by no means, a complete list of all the courses you will take, but a sampling of the major ones of interest. For a closer, more detailed look at some or all of the courses offered at your law school of choice, call and ask for a catalog of courses. The next topic of interest is the Bar Exam. In law school it was commonly referred to as "The three days from Hell." And it truly lives up to that nickname.

Chapter 9

THE BAR EXAM: The Three Days from Hell.

"Knowledge must come through action; you can have no test which is not fanciful, save by trial."

- Sophocles

First, let's begin this chapter by saying that all lawyers are members of a state Bar. There are two kinds of law studied in law school - state law and Federal law. If a lawyer attended law school in Georgia then he probably learned mostly Georgia Law. The state laws are things like divorce law, criminal law, wills, etcetera. Whereas, Federal laws are things like Federal Income Tax, Estate Tax, Bankruptcy, and the like. The state laws that are studied come from the state in which your law school is located. All states, except Louisiana, practice Old English style law. While Louisiana's state law is called Napoleonic Law and is styled after the Law of the French courts. My relative who attended Tulane Law School, which is in Louisiana, was encouraged by his family to come back home to Alabama to practice law. But the fact that he had studied under the Napoleonic rules would have made it very difficult for him to come to Alabama to practice. In other words, he would have had to take some more classes, courses, or seminars to be able to take and pass the Alabama Bar Exam.

You see, the Federal laws are the same for all states, but state laws vary from state to state based on what has been passed by their respective legislatures. For instance, returning to our discussion of the new car *lemon* law, Georgia might have a new car *lemon* law that says you have to bring the car back to the dealer within six months to get your money back. Whereas, Tennessee might have a one year limit on their version of the so-called *lemon* law. So the choice of the law school you pick should take into consideration just where (what state) you are planning to set up your practice, or to put it another way, which set of state laws you will have to learn, in order to pass the Bar Exam. It is possible to go to law school in one state and take the Bar Exam in another and still pass it. People do it all the time. But it is not as easy as it would be if your law school were in the same state. Both state and federal law are tested on the Bar Exam. But the state law that is tested is *only* the state law from *that* state, i.e. the state where the test is taken.

------------------<>--------------------<>------------------

The Bar Exam is divided into three sections, with two being given at the same time on successive days and the third smaller section being given separately at a different site. The three sections are - 1) the Multi-State or multiple choice portion, 2) the essay or written part, and 3) the Multi-state Professional Responsibility Exam (MPRE). The Multi-State or multiple choice part is given on the last Wednesday of the month in February and July nationwide. Based on the particular state in which you are taking the exam, the essay or written portion is usually given on the Monday and Tuesday prior to the Wednesday test - hence the slogan - "the three days from Hell." The third part or MPRE is generally called the "ethics" exam. It is given by a different testing company and is given nationally at different testing centers three times a year. It is a two-hour exam and asks questions relating strictly to topics like honesty, integrity, and conflicts of interest. It doesn't test your knowledge of the law and, as such, is not considered as a part of the Bar Exam, so to speak. It is generally referred to as the "Ethics Exam," but you must pass it in order to get your Bar License in any state.

------------------<>--------------------<>------------------

The Multi-State exam consists of two hundred multiple choice questions covering legal rules of subjects that are generally common in all states, such as constitutional law, torts, evidence, real property, etcetera. You will have three hours on Wednesday morning to answer 100 multiple choice questions. Then you will have three hours on Wednesday afternoon to answer another 100 multiple choice questions. The essay or written portion of the exam is given on the preceding Monday and Tuesday and tests such areas as civil procedure, equity, arbitration, punitive damages, wills, conflicts of law, negotiable instruments, Taxation, etcetera. It is a written test and will require you to give most of your answers in "brief" or essay type format.

If my memory serves me correctly, you have to score a 70% or better on the MPRE in order to pass that test. It is a two hour exam and tests only your "ethics." However, you must pass it in order to pass the Bar Exam. The grading of the Bar Exam goes like this: you have to make 70% to pass and it is made up of two sections. The multi-state (multiple-choice) portion counts 50% of your grade on the Bar Exam and your essay portion counts 50% of your grade on the Exam. So, the Monday session counts 25 percent of your grade; the Tuesday session counts 25 percent of your grade; and the Wednesday or multiple choice session counts 50 percent of your grade. A little common sense would tell you to schedule your studying and reviewing for the exam by concentrating twice as much time on the Wednesday or multiple choice portion. Think about it. It only takes a grade of 70% to pass the Bar Exam, so you could make 50% of your total grade on the Wednesday test, if you got all 200 questions right. Theoretically speaking, one could obtain an excellent grade on the Wednesday test and an excellent grade on the Tuesday test and not even bother to show up for the Monday test and still pass! It would be difficult, but it is possible. Therefore, I concentrated my study time on the multi-state part.

------------------<>--------------------<>------------------

Some of my professors told me that the Bar exam was a rite of passage more so than a true exam, and in some ways they were right. For instance, law school doesn't teach you how to pass the bar exam. And you can't retain enough of the subject matter that you learned in, say, freshman Torts class to be able to help yourself much on the bar with that Tort knowledge. But you have to have the J.D. degree to qualify to take the test. So you have to graduate law school to qualify to sit for it. Bar review courses are usually necessary in order to pass. It sounds crazy to say that most people have to go to law school for three or four years and then, still don't know enough law to be able to pass the Bar Exam, but that's the way it is. Everyone that I know, who took the bar exam when I did, that passed, had taken a Bar Exam review course. One of the reasons for this is that the Bar Exam covers topics that were studied in first and second year of school and they probably need to be refreshed in that person's memory. There are several good ones out there. One is BARBRI. One is PMBR. Some upper echelon law schools provide bar review seminars for their graduates, taught on campus by the school. Some even provide this service for free to their recent graduates. The BARBRI course emphasizes subjects covered on the written part of the exam, while PMBR concentrates on the Multi-state (multiple choice) topics. Although, I signed up for both of these, for my money, it made more sense to concentrate my time on the multi-state topics, since that was 50% of the test. The BARBRI review is a good review, for the sections covering the essay parts. However, I did not feel that I gained any advantage on the Multi-state part of the bar exam by studying the BARBRI multi-state review sessions or books.

I studied them for many days and feel that they did not help me at all. Whereas, with the PMBR, I recognized many exact fact situations in questions that I studied in their review on the exam itself. It is a tremendous help to be sitting there reading a fact situation on the Bar Exam and already have the answer memorized. The company that produces and distributes the Multi-state exam never publishes for review courses any of the questions that have been used on a previous exam, except for maybe a few that are old and won't ever be used again. So that's not much help. I've heard that some of these bar review course companies hire people to take the Bar Exam and *memorize* the questions. Then they use these fact situations in questions of their own that they prepare. The BARBRI didn't have any of these that I could tell. But, the Bar Exam had between thirty and forty questions that presented the exact same fact situations as the ones presented in some of the questions on the PMBR review. And, although, it has been a while since I took the review course and the bar exam, I'm sure that is probably still the case. To put it another way, I already had the correct answer burned into my brain on about 35 questions out of two hundred when I went in the room to take the exam. That is a very substantial number.

The contact information for these is:

BARBRI - www.BARBRI.com 1-800-777-EXAM   Approx. $2000.00 usd

PMBR - www.PMBR.com 1-310-450-8481 Approx. $300.00 usd

There are some others but these are the main two used by most students.

The application process to actually take the Bar Exam will start during your junior year. The forms that you will need to fill out are usually provided to you by your law school. The process is very personal and you will be asked questions that pry into your personal feelings and behaviors. This process is part of the screening that your state bar association will perform on you to be sure that you are "bar worthy." Your State Bar Admissions office will do a background check on you to see if you have any felony convictions. You will be fingerprinted, among other things. Your prints will be cross checked against the national fingerprint database to see if you are clean. Your family and neighbors will be interviewed about your background and character. You will be throughly checked to see if you are bar worthy. To some this feels like an invasion of their privacy, but it is just another part of the process that you must endure in order to become an attorney.

Once you have passed the background check and been scheduled to sit for the exam, you can begin your serious planning for the exam. Most everyone takes the July exam because it is right after they graduate from law school and everything is still fresh on their minds. So the number sitting for the July exam will always be greater than the number sitting for the February exam. The February exam participants are people who had a class to make up during summer school or who failed the July exam. The pass rate is usually about 50-65% no matter how many take it.

Once you have gotten your schedule for your review course(s), sit down with a calendar, and take the subjects to be reviewed and divide them up by difficulty and number of hours necessary to learn. Spread this out over the time you will have in June and July to study. Devote as much time as possible to review during this time. If you have a job, try to take some days off for this purpose. Don't get burned out, but be diligent about it. Sample exams will be provided and taking these are excellent exercises. Some of my classmates would get together at our County Law Library to study for the Bar Exam. I never attended because I study better when I'm by myself and can go at my own pace. The sample tests can be very enlightening in pointing out your weak areas. Although, most of us know just where we are weak or what areas of the law we don't like, sometimes, we have to see a test score to drive home that weakness. I personally was weak in Real Estate law, because I knew I wasn't going to ever be practicing in that area.

-------------------<>--------------------<>-------------------

The demographics for the exam will vary by state, but ours is given in Montgomery at the Civic Center. Book a motel room well in advance so that you can be sure of getting the one you want. Try to find one as close to the test site as possible. That way if you have a flat tire, dead battery or other type of malfunction to deal with one morning, you can just walk to the exam site, and still not be late. This will help to put you at ease. I stayed at the Capitol Inn, which was only about three blocks from the test site.

Don't stay with someone else. One of my classmates had an aunt who lived in Montgomery, who had invited him to stay with her during the exam. He thought he was going to save a couple hundred bucks on a room. He made the awful mistake of accepting and she spent the whole three nights catching up on *ole home week*. He didn't get any sleep. He had to eat her cooking. He had to spend his valuable study time telling her about how the wife, mother, and babies were doing. *Big mistake*. Needless to say, he flunked the exam. My friend, Robert, rode down and shared a room with one of our other classmates. That classmate's daughter had a cold. Robert caught the cold when he went by their house to pick the guy up, and spent the last two days of the exam sick as a dog. Plus, the classmate snored and Robert didn't get two good hours sleep the whole time. *Big mistake*. Stay by yourself. Run your own show. Plan ahead. I had bananas, peanut butter sandwiches, and sodas in my cooler in my car trunk in case I wanted to study during the hour and a half lunch break each day. I would walk out to the car, read my review books for the next session, review my acronyms, eat my sandwich, bananas, or snacks.

I carried plenty of pens, pencils, and two watches with me to the Exam. The essay portion must all be written in ball point pen, while the multi-state must be done in number two pencil. I bought some ball point pens that featured erasable ink and tried them out prior to going down. The requirement to write the essay portion in ball point pen and still keep your writing neat serves to add to the pressure. The erasable pens worked great. I could make a mistake, erase it and keep going without missing a beat. I carried mechanical pencils with number two lead and plenty of erasers. I had all of my pens, and paraphernalia, including my ID and admission ticket in a large clear baggie, that I left on the floor next to my chair during the exam. I, also, had cough drops, chewing gum, and peppermints in case I developed a cough. I carried a big cup of coffee with me as well. You can take your watch in with you, but they don't allow you to have a timer or watch that alarms or beeps during the exam. One guy sitting about four rows behind me had a watch that beeped every hour or so. One of the examinees sitting close to me complained to the proctor about it after the first session. The proctor reemphasized to the group that no timers/beepers/alarm clocks were allowed in the auditorium. The same watch went off again in the second session. The same person complained to the proctor again. It was distracting to everyone in our vicinity. It was not very loud but loud enough to be very distracting. The proctor scolded everyone and reminded everyone again "No alarms allowed." About an hour into the third session, the watch started beeping again. The guy who had complained got up, went over to the table where the watch was, picked up the watch, threw it on the floor, and crushed it with his boot. Several of the examinees applauded.

------------------<>--------------------<>------------------

The First Day:

The general mood and atmosphere at the initial gathering of the participants outside of the test center on the first day is grim. There are both tension and electricity in the air at the same time. Some people are studying notes. Some are feverishly smoking cigarettes. Some are pacing, but all, to the man, are nervous. You try to remain calm but you know in the back of your mind what is riding on this. You have studied and you are about as prepared as you are going to be. Some of the test sections require you to give lists of things - such as the evidence exceptions to hearsay. I created some acronyms to help me remember these and I carefully reviewed the six or seven of those that I had for the first day. After we were allowed to go inside and find our assigned seats, the sealed exam booklets and legal pads for the essay portion had been placed on the table at our assigned seats in front of us. While I was waiting for the proctor to finish her instructions and start the session, I was making tick marks on the legal pad on every other line. The essay portion has to be written double spaced. That was one of the rules. These tiny tick marks were to help me remember to double space my writing. I made them for the first ten lines or so on each new page. I, also, wrote down the acronyms just as soon as I could on the pad. That way I wouldn't risk forgetting them under pressure. You realize that there are no second chances, even though you can take the test over. About two or three years earlier, one guy had a heart attack right in the middle of the first session. Fortunately, one of the examinees was a nurse and she saved the man's life. But they wouldn't let her take that section over. She had to wait until the next bar exam, to retake that section. I thought that was a bit much, but the State Bar allows <u>no</u> exceptions.

The grading of the test takes about three months, so if you fail you don't have much time to study for the next one. The bar examiners do this by design because they know that you don't want to keep studying and taking these review courses if you passed it. So, they know that you won't study until you get your results. Then again, most people come out of the exam feeling like they failed it. So, even if you think you failed it, how stupid would it be to start studying for it again only to find out that you passed. When you do get your results, you will either be very happy or know it's time to start all over again with the review. If you didn't pass, though, don't give up. It's easier to pass the second time around because you know exactly what to expect.

-------------------<>--------------------<>------------------

The Test Sessions:

The first day, in my opinion was by far the toughest, because you really didn't know what to expect. The second and third day were not as nerve racking to me because, I had a better feel of what to expect and how to pace myself on my answers. The first day for the Alabama Essay exam, which by the way has adopted some of the national bar exam essay procedures, consists of two sessions on civil litigation, civil procedure, equity, arbitration, punitive damages, and several other subjects.

The second day, which is, also, essay, consisted of negotiable instruments, conflicts of law, U.C.C., secured transactions, wills and trusts. The third day is the multiple choice section (called multi-state) - made up of 100 questions during the morning session which is three hours, and the afternoon session which was made up of 100 questions during another three hour session.

I had different strategies for each day, but the one thing that probably helped me more than anything else I did, was to make word acronyms out of the first letters of the things that had many different parts. For instance, some of the exceptions to the exclusion of hearsay evidence are *present state of (m)ind, (e)xcited utterance, present sense (I)mpression, declaration of (p)hysical condition, statement of (p)ersonal history, (o)fficial records, etc.* I came up with POMPEI as my acronym and burned it into my memory. When I started to take that section of the test I would immediately write down my acronyms as soon as time to begin was called. I, also, knew how long I had to finish each section and tried to help myself stay on pace to be able to finish. For instance, on the multi-state I knew I had 180 minutes to answer 100 questions, and let's say that the time to begin was called at exactly 9 a.m. and would be over at exactly 12 noon, - I would turn to question number 33 in my test booklet and write 10:00 o'clock next to it. Then I would turn to question number 66 and write 11:00 o'clock next to it. Then when I got to that question I could check myself to see how my pace was and if I needed to speed up. The answers to the multiple-choice questions had to be penciled in on the separate answer sheet by darkening in the proper circle for a, b, c, or d. I would mark my answers by circling the right answer on the booklet and then about every 30 questions I would stop my reading and answering and go back and darken in the answers on the answer sheet. This saved some time, if you went to the separate answer sheet after each question to mark it, you wasted three to five seconds finding the place on the answer sheet and then more time finding your place back on the question booklet. By marking them all at one time I would not get out of sequence and I could mark one right after another. I worked out the math after the morning session and calculated that that process alone saved me over nine minutes. That could mean another five questions that I would have time to read and answer on the morning and another five on the afternoon session.

Another trick that I learned worked quite well. The multiple choice questions all gave a short fact situation and then you had four or five questions to answer about the facts in that paragraph. I would take each question as I came to it and quickly survey that fact question to see if it was a long fact situation and if it was on real property. Real property was my weakest subject in law school, if you recall. I did not review very much real estate during the review courses. I, pretty much, just wrote those off. If the question was a long question and was on real property I would skip it and go back to it if I had time at the end of that session. Many of the real property questions were long, so this worked to my advantage giving me more time to study and answer questions that I had a better chance of getting right. If I didn't have time to go back and read these, I would go back and mark the *longest* answer of the four choices on each question without reading it. I had taken several statistics courses in college and even taught Business Statistics I & II at the college level, previously. So, I performed my own statistical analysis on about half of the sample test questions that were on the BARBRI & PMBR reviews. The answer that was the *longest* of the four choices was right about 38% of the time. So by marking the *longest answer*, this raised the possibility of guessing a right answer from 25 to 38 per cent on the ones that I didn't know or didn't have time to read, if the bar exam held true to form.

I know that not all examinees will be able to use all of these tips. However, if there is just one of these that will cause you to get one more question correct, then it was worth reading. So good luck with your exam and I hope that you get the highest score in the state when you take it. Now, we begin our discussion of that dreaded four letter word - *WORK*. With the Bar Exam out of the way it is now time to go to work. This next chapter begins the discussion of the preparation phase for this.

Chapter 10

YOU'VE PASSED THE BAR:
Now you're *really* scared!

O let us love our occupations,
Bless the squire and his relations,
Live upon our daily rations,
And always know our proper stations.

Chs. Dickens - The Chimes, Second Quarter

Passing the Bar Exam was the easy part. Establishing a law practice is what really checks a person's metal. Passing the Bar Exam takes about six months, while establishing a law practice can, sometimes, take a lifetime. Let me give you an example. There is a thing called the indigent list that attorneys apply for that allows them to be appointed by the state judge to defend criminal defendants who are indigent (i.e., can't afford to hire their own lawyer) and the state pays the lawyer an hourly rate to defend these people. There is a local attorney who previously had an office in my office building. He graduated from the most prestigious law school in Alabama more than thirty years ago. And, he is still on that indigent appointee list. He still *needs* the money, and this is not uncommon.

Now, if you have a father or some other relative who will accept you into their practice, then many of the heartaches and problems that are spelled out in this book can be avoided. But, if you are like most of us and you don't have someone like this to take you in, then you might be like most new lawyers - the first person in your family to become an attorney. Trying to begin your practice as a sole practitioner is not an easy way to go. The ideal situation would be to have an established firm "hire" you and train you - bring you along slowly - as an "apprentice" lawyer. That way you have people you can ask about certain procedural rules and situations that arise on a daily basis. This way you don't get kicked in the teeth as much by the opposition. But finding a firm to "hire" you is a very difficult task. Less than 10 percent of the ninety or so of my fellow law school classmates were successful in doing this. There are many reasons behind this. First, most attorneys feel that there are too many lawyers practicing law now. You would be asking them for a job and they already view you as competition and are, in no way, going to share some of their business with you. My county has a population of 110,000 and has one hundred fifty six licensed attorneys. *All* attorneys feel that the market for attorneys is already overly saturated, and getting worse. The main reason behind this is, as we have previously discussed, too many people decide they want to become attorneys *without knowing anything about the job and even less about the market for attorneys.* So from the very beginning, you are the enemy - competing with all the other attorneys in your circuit for a limited amount of attorney fees to be had.

Sure, you might have graduated from law school and passed the Bar, but you probably already know that law school didn't really prepare you to pass the Bar, much less, prepare you to practice law. I mean, whoever heard of a law school having something like a "LAW 101 - Basic Lawyering Skills" course. Mine didn't and yours won't either. So where does that leave those of us who didn't know ANYTHING about the actual practice of law? When I received my admission certification from the Alabama Supreme Court, I was hoping that it would have some *instructions* with it. No luck there either. Unfortunately, when you start the practice of law, you're on your own. You have to accept that as the beginning *standard* and go from there. As noted in the first chapter, when you first begin to practice, you may think that practicing law is a *noble* profession. However, it is extremely important that you learn first and foremost that practicing law is a **BUSINESS** and if you don't approach your practice from that point of view, you aren't going to be around long enough to find out if it's a noble profession or not. It could be that you made straight "A"s; graduated Order of the Coif; were editor of your school Law Journal; and are the legal researcher from Hell; -- but if you can't pay the phone bill, you can't practice law! Historically, having to deal, on a daily basis, with scummy clients, heavy debt load from student loans, pressure, long hours, constant "Lawyer jokes," and the financial uncertainties of not having a regular paycheck causes many attorneys to just give it up, as was the case with some of my law school classmates.

One lady attorney began to practice in my circuit about the same time I did. She was not a former student at BSL, but had graduated from one of the best law schools in the country, the same year I did. She was smart, pretty, articulate, and well prepared. An established, local law firm hired her to be an "apprentice" lawyer in their firm. They had her begin by getting on the indigent criminal list. She decided after about two months that she didn't like dealing with scum-bag criminals on a daily basis and they let her change her practice to juvenile work. That lasted about three months. She, then, decided to try domestic relations practice, but the clients that she represented would call at all hours of the night to cry to her about the other spouse acting like an ass-hole, and couldn't she make them stop acting that way. About seven or eight months after she began to practice, I saw her at a docket call. She looked like she had been sick. Some of her hair had fallen out, and she had lost about 30 pounds. She looked rough. About two months later, she had a nervous breakdown and quit practicing. Her husband was stuck with paying more than sixty thousand dollars of her student loans. She found out the hard way what most potential law students don't know, and that is - it seems the Judges are against you, especially if you are unprepared, and they are willing to embarrass you on a moment's notice, even in front of your clients; the lawyers on the other side are cutthroat right from the start, - they treat you as though you are their direct competition, because you are; they hate you, and would love for you to quit your practice so there will be more business for them; your clients don't want to cooperate - they want you to do what *they* want and to do it now! - to heck with procedure, the law, or rules; the list of adverse conditions and factors goes on and on.

The most pitiful example of this conflicted job predicament for attorneys happened in an incident with one of my former classmates about eight years after I began to practice. I had signed up several thousand claimants for the PCB contamination case against Monsanto, and had gone to Birmingham to meet with the large firm that I had associated to help me prosecute the case. One of the lead lawyers and I had gone to lunch at a local Bar B Q joint. We had both just finished a Bar B Q plate special. My head was down as the section waiter for that section asked us if we enjoyed our food. I thought that his voice sounded familiar. I looked up and it was "John" a good friend of mine from law school. During law school, he was a manager for one of the big DHR departments for the State. He had roughly 200 employees who worked for him. He had a job with extensive responsibility, and an excellent income. He had a BS in Psychology and a Master's degree in counseling. He quit his job with the state as soon as he passed the Bar Exam and opened his law practice in Bessemer. I said "John! Is that you?" His face turned red and he was visibly embarrassed. He was one of the most vocal of my classmates when he was in law school about the ass that he was going to kick when he became an attorney. He began to rationalize the fact that he couldn't make it in practice. After six years of practice, he had - closed his practice; unsuccessfully tried to get his job back with the state; gotten divorced; and was now working as a waiter in a Bar B Q joint. He looked rough. When I was at the Court House in Anniston some weeks later and told one of my other classmates of seeing "John" and that he was now a waiter, they couldn't believe it. He was a good guy and I hated the fact that I had embarrassed him that day just by chance by sitting in his section.

-------------------<>--------------------<>-------------------

The first three months after you graduate can be the most discouraging for the recent graduate. Let me explain just what I mean by that. There were eight people who graduated law school, who were in my class and who were from my Circuit. Of that eight, one started driving to another Circuit to practice on the indigent team. (I'll call him *Alpha*.) Alpha told me that he wanted to practice in a different Circuit because he knew that he was going to screw up a lot and he didn't want to be embarrassed in front of his friends. He made about $3,600 that first year, and eventually quit that Circuit because he felt that the DA was going to set him up by planting some dope in his car, because he would never accept a reasonable plea for his clients. The second classmate I'll call *Bravo*. Bravo went from law office to law office applying for a "job" as lawyer trainee. There were a dozen or so firms in town with multiple attorney members. They all laughed at him. He, later, worked out a deal with an attorney to "work for his rent." Bravo has now been practicing over eleven years and has been with five different firms during that time. Keep in mind as I go through these, that none of these classmates had tried to get an attorney "job" prior to passing the Bar Exam. It seems like they all knew in the back of their minds that they *could* flunk the exam and then they would be embarrassed and unemployed again. The third classmate I'll call *Charlie*. She went from law firm to law firm as well, and eventually got a job doing real property title searches for one of the firms in town. You could drive by the Probate Judge's office for the first two or three years that she was in practice and see her car parked in her usual parking place. The fourth classmate I'll call *Delta*. She had a job working with the District Attorney's bad check unit prior to starting to law school. So she was able to get a job working with the DA as an assistant DA after she passed the bar. The fifth classmate I'll call *Echo*. She opened her practice as a solo practice in a town of about 4,000 population, outside of Anniston but still in our Circuit. She stayed in practice there for less than two years, closed that office, and moved to Anniston. She has changed firms two or three times since then. The sixth classmate I'll call *Foxtrot*. Foxtrot opened his office in a rural community of about 300 people, Southeast of Anniston. He has since closed that office and moved his solo practice to Anniston in an old building that was formerly an auto repair shop, located close to the Calhoun County Jail. The seventh classmate, I'll call *Quebec*. Quebec interviewed with about ten firms, after he passed the Bar and they all laughed at him. He then rented a back room in the office of a local CPA. I saw him taking two of his clients in his car to the court house recently. His car is about twenty years old, has a cracked windshield, no air conditioner, and was smoking so bad that I saw the clients coughing.

The eighth classmate is me. Of these eight, one is now a District Judge, four have divorced their spouse, at least one has filed bankruptcy, and one has passed away. This group could be and probably is a typical group of beginning "new" lawyers.

At times, I have called the office of a local attorney and gotten a phone company message that the phone had been temporarily disconnected. The competition is so stiff that you are forced to take cases that you know will drive you crazy. Is this sounding like fun to you? If you are still convinced that this career is for you, then you need to begin diligently practicing your "***chicken***" skills. You remember those don't you, from Chapter 2? It's called the ability to "make chicken salad out of chicken shit."

Chapter 11

SETTING UP SHOP: Where to Begin

"Some are born great, some achieve greatness, and some have greatness thrust upon them."
Shakespeare -Twelfth Night.

The very first step in setting up your practice is picking a city in which to practice. This is the first and always the easiest step, because everyone knows which city they like even before they graduate from law school. Next is to find an office. And let me stop right here and say that not all of the ideas and suggestions offered in this treatise will fit each person's individual needs. So, based on the size of the city in which you decide to practice, you may have to go to Plan B or even C or D. The general location of the office should be determined within certain parameters. Before you begin looking, have a budgeted amount in mind for rent. And always rent. I have seen Attorneys who didn't believe in paying rent - build an office, only to find that they used up too much of their operating capital and became strapped to survive it. I've seen several file bankruptcy because of this very decision. With a dollar figure in mind as to the amount, we begin as to what our office preferences should be.

1) Pick a lawyer to be your "Mentor," but don't let him/her know it. And then try to get a suitable office in the same building as his office, and preferably next door. In picking a lawyer mentor (LM), choose someone who is a friend, or if that's not possible, someone who is a friend of your family. If that's not possible then you may have to "buy" yourself an LM. And I'll explain that in a minute. In all cases, choose someone who has at least five years of practice experience and who, also, specializes in an area of the law that doesn't interest you. If you are going to do mostly criminal work, pick someone in real estate, or vice versa. This will help him/her to feel that you are not in direct competition with him for clients, thereby creating a much more positive work relationship. If you don't know anyone that you can pick as your LM, you may have to "buy" one. By this I mean, find a suitable office on a floor next to a lawyer that fits the above criteria but who is only an acquaintance, preferably a lawyer that has a conference room. Go to him before you sign any lease and tell him who you are and what is your area(s) of concentration, so that he will be more comfortable with your possible presence next door. Explain to him that you are thinking about renting the office next door and would he be interested in allowing you to use his copier and occasionally his conference room - by appointment only of course - for a monthly fee of say 50 - 75 bucks. He will think that's a good deal, since no one can do $50 worth of copying in a month. Don't be cheap about it, $75 is not too much. This money you pay him can't help but make him feel somewhat obligated to you since it's a good bit more than his cost. Therefore, you will then be able to feel free to ask him any and all the questions you like during lunch or while getting coffee. In some cases, but not that often, you will need advice from someone in your area of speciality. At times like this, call an attorney in that specialty or research it on line. Conversely, what you will need on an almost daily basis is an attorney, i.e., your LM, that you can ask general, vanilla questions about things such as procedure and fee prices. Keep in mind that this is stuff

that you would know yourself through osmosis after a year or two. But sometimes it will be extremely important to have this <u>immediate</u> access to this type information available. An example might help. Let's say that today is Thursday and you have been sitting in your office since Monday with no clients coming in. You NEED money. All of sudden, an unannounced potential client comes in and asks if you would do a Quit Claim Deed for him. You know how to do that and, you know that the standard form for that is in the forms book and you can get a copy of it off the computer CD in about two minutes. So you tell him "Yes." And then he asks "How much will it cost me?" This being the first one you ever did, you say to yourself "Good question!" You know at this point that you have to give him a price. If your price is too high, he'll tell everyone you're a crook. And if its too low, he'll tell everyone you don't know what you're doing. At which point you now have three choices:

a) Tell him you're sorry but you forgot that you don't do quit claim deeds.

b) Roll the dice and give him a price, hoping you will be close.

c) Ask him for his drivers license - saying that you always make a copy to put in the case file. He'll say "Sure." You take it next door to LM's office to copy. At which time you ask LM or LM's secretary - "How much do you charge for a quit claim deed?"

Number three is the only good option and it will not be available if you don't have an LM close by or at least close enough that you can sneak out and call. Options one and two expose you to lost revenue and possibly lost reputation. This LM idea will save you many, many problems when you are first beginning to practice. My LM was a local attorney who practiced about 95 percent real estate law, and I wanted no part of that. He had been practicing about 20 years and helped me tremendously with my initial learning curve into the practice of law.

2) Get an office close to the Courthouse, or at least within walking distance. This will save you some grief, if you ever have car trouble, forget something, or some such other problem and have a court case. Plus your secretary can walk to the Courthouse to file things for you.

3) Get an office in a bank or professional building. If there is a professional office complex mall close by that is also a good choice. Shared secretary, office machines, and conference rooms offer a lot of utility, at an inexpensive price.

4) A small office in a bank or professional building close to the Courthouse is much better than a beautiful large office in an old renovated house on the outskirts of town. Take the small office and fix it up. Many times you can buy a can of paint and do the work yourself and save some serious rent. Small is always better when starting out. It costs less to furnish; less for the rent; and all you need is room for you and a secretary.

5) My first office was in a bank building and two blocks or less from the post office, the Courthouse, Federal Building, a five and dime, my favorite men's clothing store, supermarket with deli, two saloons, drugstore, both of my banks, two therapeutic massage businesses, and several nice restaurants.

6) If the bank where you locate your office just so happens to, also, be a bank where your family or your spouse's family have their accounts and/or loans that will be a big plus for you, also. Make fast friends with a loan officer if you haven't already. Buy him some lunches and ask about his available services for small businesses.

7) Some *new* lawyers make the mistake of agreeing to perform legal work for another attorney in exchange for office rent. This always turns out to be a disaster. Do not fall into this trap. Sometimes an attorney will have some vacant rooms or spaces in his office due to someone quitting, retiring, or whatever. And it is extremely tempting when you see this ready-made office, complete with secretarial help, to want

to just move right in. It seems, at first blush, like this would be an ideal setup. You would have a LM, a secretary, a conference room, and an office, all for just helping out and giving some of your time to your LM. You know you are going to have plenty of time, without a case load of your own to work on, that you could use to help him. Well, it's not quite that way. Let's look at the issues in this scenario that *don't* work. First, it's good that he could be your LM and help train you. But, the work that he is going to give you to do for him is work that is too hard for the secretary to do. And any time he has a Court hearing, client meeting or situation that he has to attend where he is going to get his butt chewed out, he is going to send you in his place. He will think nothing of sending you 300 miles in one day to deliver a subpoena. There will be times that arise after you have been in this type situation for a few months where you will have conflicts with his assignments for you and your own clients' appointments for your practice. He will invariably come up with an emergency problem that you have to take care of for him. If you refuse he can kick you out. If you don't refuse you lose your client and have animosity toward the LM. These are both lose-lose situations. His workload for you will slowly expand to completely fill your 40 hour week.

This situation (working for your rent) back-fires every time. In fact, I have never seen it work out where both parties parted as friends. If you feel that logistically and socially moving into a vacant office with a lawyer like this is good for you in most of the other advantageous areas we have already discussed above, then do so, but do so under a fixed agreement with that person. Tell him that you will have time to help him, but that you are going to charge a fixed hourly rate, and stick to that rate. Also, have him set a fixed monthly rate for your amount of the rent. You can still trade off, on paper, the amount you owe him against what he owes you, but the barter would always be an exact dollar amount and neither person would ever be able to feel he was being taken advantage of.

8) What about furnishings? Keep in mind that you need to keep an eye on costs, so the furnishing for your office need to be nice but not expensive. Don't go out and buy a bunch of furniture on credit. The payments will hinder your practice over time. Get your relatives to let you scour their attics and basements for old furniture you can borrow and/or buy that might help you. Coffee tables, end tables, high back chairs, - all can help in a waiting room. Talk to your loan officer/banker. Banks are always updating and remodeling. I bought a secretary's desk, credenza, two high back chairs, a nice leather executive chair, and some other items out of my bank's basement surplus for about $50.00 a piece. The desk and credenza had scratches on them but I took a bottle of brown shoe polish and fixed them so you could not tell them from new. I, also, was able to borrow a really good electric typewriter that they had upgraded, thereby saving about $500.00. Another great idea is law books. They really help give a professional look to your office. So, anytime a lawyer dies, retires, or is moving his office, ask for any surplus law books that he might have. Also, ask any other lawyers that upgrade their books on an annual basis if you can have their old volumes. Even books that will never be used in your practice can help cover a bare wall and make your office *look* professional. A new attorney that has an office full of law books appears to have experience, even if he doesn't. If you happen to locate a furniture piece that really, really looks good and you feel it will add a real touch of class to your office, but the piece is expensive - go ahead and buy it. If your clients think you paid big money for some of your furnishings, then they will probably think you paid big money for all your furnishings. Another trick is to take some old clothes that you don't want anymore to donate to the local thrift store and check out their furniture while you're there. If you are afraid someone will see you and blow your image, go to the thrift stores that are in the other cities that you have to travel to from time to time. That way no one will see you that knows you. I, also, bought some of my best suits from thrift stores and had them resized thereby

saving thousands of dollars right off the bat. Some of them still had the original price tags on them. I have bought brand names suits at thrift stores that cost me less than what I had to pay to get them fitted and dry-cleaned. I didn't have but two suits when I passed the bar and I had paid retail for both. By utilizing thrift stores, I now have about twenty five more suits and have less invested in them combined than I did in the other two. Ties are another area where you can make a good impression for a small investment. Check out the ties while you are at the thrift store. Ties are not expensive, and wearing a different tie each day, even when you wear the same suit, gives you a fresh sense of fashionability and variety in your attire and thereby promotes your professionalism.

9) Secretaries: One of the most expensive items that you will be faced with is employee expense. Having a secretary is a double edged sword. Payroll will always be the most expensive item in your annual budget. However, some excellent, common sense options are available to help with this. Paying a full-time secretary minimum wage will cost you over $ 11,000 per year or a little over $ 916 per month. That amount would make a nice house payment. So how you pick and choose your hired help is a major concern from a budgeting stand-point when you are first beginning to practice. The advantages of having a secretary are many, while there are only a couple of disadvantages. The main disadvantage is the cost. Another is, if you hire one that's incompetent and don't monitor her work very closely she could get you in trouble and even disciplined by the Bar. And it's hard, if not impossible, to find a good one that will work for minimum wage. So, let me start out by saying that as a new lawyer you don't have to have a secretary. You can get by with answering your own phone, and doing your own typing. But hiring a secretary, if approached properly, can be one of your biggest assets when starting out. Let's go down the list of why this is.

Hiring a secretary costs money, so you need to get the best bang for your buck. Having a person to answer the phone is a plus for your professionalism even if she doesn't perform any other tasks. But this is not as important as keeping the doors open, and sometimes spending what little fees that are coming in on a secretary won't make any sense. So, what to do. Opt for a part time secretary to start with. Having one come in for two afternoons a week is not very expensive and it gives you some flexibility. For instance, if you are on the indigent list and the Criminal Court meets every Friday afternoon then scheduling her to come in on Friday afternoon works well so she can cover the office phone calls on the Fridays that you are in court. Also, when clients call and want an appointment, you can schedule their appointments on the afternoons that she will be there. And, since your clients usually only come to see you by appointment, they will think that you have a secretary, period. Another trick is to have her record the voice mail message that plays when someone calls and you are on the phone or not in the office. Most law offices nowadays, even the big firms, use automated phone call handling methods so using one in your practice that doesn't just sound like an answering machine will work just fine. As your practice grows you can increase the hours that she works to be proportional to your needs.

Now, how do we find someone to handle this part time job? The local state employment office will have a list of candidates for you to interview. They have a fairly good screening process and they don't charge a finder's fee. So you might want to try there. Another source that is an excellent way to go is getting in touch with the local Community College and/or Trade School. They always have an Office Administration program for the secretarial students. Many times they are looking for businesses to Co-Op and will send over students- bright, intelligent students - for you to interview and hire, that only require you grading them at the end of their term. That means their services for two to three afternoons a week are *FREE* for a whole semester. If you like their work, you can hire them to come in the other two days for minimum wage, thereby having a secretary every afternoon of the week for only about $50.00. Some *high schools* even have vocational programs that offer this same type of set up, where the employee works for their grade for the semester. Whichever method you use to pick the persons to interview, be sure to give them a test. Have them type a short letter on the computer. I tell them that I don't care how long it takes them to type it, just as long as it has NO errors. Then, I secretly time them to see how long they take.

Another thing to consider when hiring a secretary is to understand that you might be able to hire someone who had previously worked as a legal secretary, had quit to have babies and now would like a part time job since the kids have started to school. This option would cost you more on an hourly basis but many of these types are really *fast* and can do more in three hours than some people can in three days. They might, also, if they are good enough, act as your Lawyer Mentor in a pinch. I found one like this. She was a legal secretary for a large local firm for 15 years, and now only wanted to work part time. She could literally type 120 words a minute with no errors. This really worked out great for both of us and she worked for me until her husband retired from his job about two or three years later. When I first began to practice, she could knock out a whole week's worth of work for me in about two hours. And although she was not cheap, she was well worth what I paid her since she was fast, excellent with grammar and spelling, knew a lot about the Law, and only wanted to work part time. And last but not least, ALWAYS, hire someone who is computer literate even if you're not. This is a must in today's legal environment, if for no other reason because many Courts now require that their Court's filings be done electronically. The U.S. Federal Bankruptcy Courts and the U.S. District Courts now require all filings to be electronic and unless someone in your office is computer literate you are going to be at a huge disadvantage. These are just some of the hints and tricks that I found to be helpful during my first three or four years of practice.

This next chapter will examine some of the things that have been mentioned in the previous chapters relating to the wide spread discontent among some present-day attorneys, and how you can avoid some of the same possible pit-falls in your own practice.

Chapter 12

THE LAWYER LANDSCAPE:
Why the Hate?

There is no duty we so much underrate as the duty of being happy.
Robert Louis Stevenson

Over 36 percent of the people who were in my law school graduating class have already quit the practice of law. Within five years of graduation, the ones who had quit, and the ones who have publicly admitted hating the practice of law, constituted over 60 percent of the class. I'm sure that the percentage is higher than that, because some of the graduates probably do not feel comfortable admitting that they really don't enjoy their chosen "noble" profession. It's hard for someone to admit that they made a major mistake in choosing a career, especially, when all of their peers think that their career carries the *"mystique."* This is all too common with lawyers, and if they hate practicing, you might too. So, read on. My class is not atypical in its' disdain for this kind of work. At first, I was having a difficult time understanding all this unhappiness since I thoroughly enjoyed my practice. (I should note here that I had other business interests and other sources of income.) These bad attitudes were very puzzling to say the least. Perhaps it was just my approach. At the risk of being mistaken about all of this, I decided to see if, in fact, it was really that bad. I began to pursue some statistics on the members of the Alabama Bar from the state bar office of admissions. Could it be possible that it was just the lawyers from my Circuit or just the lawyers from my law school who were hating it?

The investigation proved to be very interesting. As of August 2005, the numbers provided by the membership office of the Alabama State Bar consisted of the following: 14,815 persons had passed the Bar Exam, been admitted, and are still alive. Of that number, 120 have been disbarred, and 30 are on disability status. But the most striking number that appeared was the number who had passed the bar and have now chosen NOT to practice - that number was 5,764. Of course, of this number, some are retirees. Ironically, even with the retirees excluded, that still calculates out to be approximately 40 percent of the total. Forty percent of all Alabama attorneys have chosen, either voluntarily, involuntarily, or for whatever reason, NOT to practice. Could it be possible that it was just the lawyers in Alabama who were unhappy with it? To be sure, I decided to check the Georgia State Bar, too. The numbers there were just as disheartening. As of August 2005, the active number was 28,781. While the number, including retirees, who do not practice was 10,158. That's a little over 35%. So, my suspicions about the disdain for the practice were correct. Keep in mind that these figures do not include *any* of the practicing attorneys who hate their work. So, it would not be much of a stretch to think that probably upwards of 60 percent or more of the lawyer population wish that they had chosen some other way to make a living.

The extent of the decline in satisfaction with the profession is alarming to many young lawyers. In some ways, they feel vulnerable to these types of statistics and are frightened that they might end up in the same sad shape as some of their peers. It scares them. So much so that they won't even listen to these horror stories about practicing law while they are still in law school. They don't know anything about practicing law and they know even less about why these "good, energetic, young" lawyers would want to quit. And they won't admit that they might be wrong about their choice of a profession. They always rationalize when they hear one of these horror stories and want to think that that case was just an exception and that the dissatisfaction is not widespread. But, that is just another example of their not checking into the profession and, thereby, forming the wrong opinion about the "job."

As if these statistics didn't prove to be bad enough, the pressures of going to law school, and trying to support a family and/or maintain a good home life, as well, resulted in many of my law school classmates becoming divorced either during or shortly after law school. As I mentioned in Chapter 10, there were eight students who were in my law school graduating class who practice in this circuit. One has passed away, and four are now divorced. That leaves myself and two others who are still married to the same spouse. Most of us held full-time jobs and went to law school at night. We went to school five nights a week and then spent weekends studying and writing briefs. This left very little time for family, and it took its toll on everyone.

------------------<>--------------------<>------------------

On the brighter side, the patterns of behavior that cause a lot of the burnout are easy to avoid if you can recognize them early in your practice. What follows is a collection of useful ideas and suggestions from practicing attorneys who share some of the problem avoidance skills that they have learned during their years of practice. These suggestions are not and should not be considered as a cure all or a safe haven umbrella, but a source of tips and hints that when used with a little common sense will provide you with a stronger ability to weather some of the extreme conditions that confront new lawyers and still come out on top. So, if you're scared, say scared, and read on.

Needless to say, the financial resources available to the people who read this book will vary greatly, but keep in mind that *everyone*, rich or poor, young or old, who starts a new practice has NO experience, and some of the techniques given here could allow that person to gain a distinct advantage, both in attitude and financially over someone who doesn't know as much. Many people are afraid to go solo, but I've always been solo and it can be very rewarding if you will apply a little intelligence and are not afraid to learn from your own mistakes or, more preferably, the mistakes of others.

------------------<>-------------------<>------------------

It is now time to discuss why there is so much discontent with the "job" of attorney. We have explored some of the reasons, in passing, in some of the previous chapters. Discussing these in detail will allow you a better understanding of why the *hate* occurs. Some of these, you can do nothing about because they are just a part of the legal landscape, but some can be changed or modified in the way they will impact your practice. Here are some of the major factors that cause this massive discontent:

1)<u>Market Saturation:</u>

This issue impacts many things within the law practice framework. A quick look at an article about lawyers in the 03/05/06 issue of *PARADE* magazine shows that there are more than a *million* lawyers in the U.S. That works out to be one for every 274 people. Conversely, China only has one for every 12,745 people. On the other hand the Chinese don't have car wrecks, so much as bicycle, rickshaw, and water buffalo collisions. As bad as it looks for the over crowding of the lawyer market in Alabama, I guess it could be worse. That same *PARADE* article said Washington, D.C. has one lawyer for every 14 residents! This over crowding of the lawyer market cannot be changed overnight, but I feel that it can be changed over time through knowledge and books such as this one. First, let's look at some reasons why the market for lawyers is saturated.

We live in a free society where a person is allowed to pick their own occupation, within limits. And as I have stated so emphatically before many, many individuals decide that they want to be a lawyer without knowing anything about the legal profession. To put it another way, as a result of their watching a good *L.A.Law* episode on television five years ago, we now have another person who has just passed the bar exam and is beginning to practice law. Can you see how shallow this reasoning is? When a person has had childhood cancer, survived and decided that they wanted to become a doctor to help other kids with that disease, then that is a *chosen* profession. But deciding to become a lawyer because you were impressed with how *Ben Matlock* figured out who killed the butler on a Wednesday night episode several years ago just doesn't get it as to a *reason* to go into the law.

I have examined some of the application processes for law schools in my state and others, and some do not even ask "*Why* do you want to be an attorney?" This is a dishonor to the legal profession. Every potential law school student should be asked why they want to become an attorney on their law school application and denied admission if they cannot give a *legitimate* reason. They should be required to write an essay on that question and that essay should be given as much weight, if not more, than the LSAT score they obtained. This would be a good first step at rectifying this over-crowded market travesty. Another good step would be for all law schools to require prospective students to read this book! But I know that ain't gonna happen because their enrollment would suffer.

The end result of this lack of knowledge and lack of purpose in these students' pursuit of this occupation has a threefold negative effect upon the profession. First, there is only so much money to be had in any particular Circuit for legal fees during a year's time. There are only X number of suits to be filed. In our county, there are 156 attorneys from which a potential client might choose. If another person passes the bar exam and comes to our Circuit to practice then my chance of getting picked as the attorney for his given case goes down from 1 in 156 to 1 in 157. That doesn't sound like much but, over time, the whole county bar association suffers from lack of business. Even the attorneys that have been practicing a long time and have a well-established practice have noticed the drop in business due to the number of new attorneys.

In our Circuit in 2004, there were 20,606 filings of complaints, modifications, criminal cases, juvenile, divorce, etc. With the clerk's help, this number was analyzed and determined to be 12,009 after subtracting out all cases that were not represented by an attorney. That is to say, any case that the filer handled himself - *pro se* - we call it, and any where there was more than one criminal charge that was handled as an added offense. Using this as a general barometer to measure the Court climate in our Circuit for paid attorney fees, we can estimate that if each one of these cases paid an average of $500 then the clients' monies available to be spent on lawyer fees in our Circuit during that year at the Circuit/District level was $6,004,500. Also, keep in mind that this figure does not include any monies for Federal cases such as Bankruptcy or probate cases such as deeds, etc. Now, that sounds like a lot of fees, but if we divide that out to an average for the Circuit, that equals $38,490 per attorney for the year. Some might argue that $500 for an average fee is too low. But at least half of these cases pay less than $500, while some clients don't pay at all. So, $500 is a fair guess. Furthering this analysis, an attorney who is practicing as a sole practitioner, who employs a full time secretary that is paid $ 8.50 per hour, and who, also, pays office rent of $ 500 per month, has standing expenses of about $25,000 per year. So, if we take just those expenses away from this $38,490, we are left with $13,490 for the attorney, which computes to be $6.49 per hour which is less than he pays his secretary. Now, at the end of the year, if he were to sit down and analyze how he did that year, he would realize that he went to college and then law school for seven hard years only to wind up making less than his secretary who has only a high school diploma. This is very discouraging.

Secondly, the lack of new, good cases causes the local attorneys to be forced to take cases that lack merit. Recall the case where the lady sued McDonald's because she spilled the coffee and it burned her? These type cases always seem to make the newspaper headlines and result in the public getting a bad impression of lawyers and their creditability. Attorneys don't necessarily want to take these cases, but many times they don't have any choice if they want to keep their office doors open. This results in what some of our local judges have called the "shotgun" approach to filing suits. At least one local attorney that I know, quit practicing in our Circuit because the judges got so tired of his frivolous suits that he couldn't get a decent call from *any* judge on *any* objection in court in *any* of his cases. In all the cases that he would file, the opposing side always got the benefit of the doubt from the judge, simply because this attorney had filed so many suits that the judges thought were frivolous, that they became tired of it.

The filing of frivolous suits has gotten so bad that many new laws have been passed by Congress and the state legislatures to try to stem the tide. A recent Alabama law forces the person (plaintiff) who brings the suit to pay the legal fees of the other side (defendant) if a settlement offer is rejected by the plaintiff and the court finds at trial for less than the amount of that offer. That has helped slow down the filing of these type cases, but other laws are needed. Years ago, when anyone filed a "slip and fall" case against WalMart, WalMart would always pay a small settlement so the case would just go away, and so WalMart wouldn't have to incur any legal fees. Nowadays, WalMart doesn't pay *any* settlements for slip & fall. They try *all* of these type cases, because so many cases that lacked merit were being filed against them.

The third thing to come out of this flooding of the attorney market has been the increase in advertising by attorneys. Having too many attorneys in the market, means that attorneys will try almost anything to try to increase their business. You can't turn on the TV anymore without seeing numerous ads for lawyers. The yellow pages in the phone book have more attorney ads than any other category, including restaurants. This tends to give attorneys an "ambulance chaser" type of profile in the eyes of the public. Additionally, this advertising is not cheap and it squeezes the lawyer's budget even tighter. The result is decreased moral all the way around. Bad cases, bad clients, expensive ads to pay for, too much competition, bad public image, and sporadic income that increases the financial pressure on an attorney to a level that many times becomes unbearable.

2) Bad Cases:

Partially because of this overcrowded market the attorney has to sign up clients who have "loser" cases just to make ends meet. This breeds contempt from the beginning for both the attorney and client. The end result being that no matter how hard the attorney tries to win the case, the result is always a losing effort. The client is not satisfied with the attorney. And in most of these type of cases, the effort spent on the case is substantially more than would have been necessary on a good "winner" case. If the lawyer didn't get his money up front or took the case on a percentage, then he lost money on the case. So, he spent a lot of time; took grief from all sides; in some instances, even the Judge jumps on him for the case being so weak; and he winds up not getting any money for his efforts. The attorney's morale suffers, his bank account suffers, his reputation suffers because he lost the case, and last, his client wants to sue him for malpractice because he told the client that it was a "good" case when he initially took it.

3) Lack of Money:

The legal profession, pretty much, requires that you have an office. It also requires that you dress the part. And you can't take your client to the Court House to try his million-dollar case in your car that has a trash bag for a back window on the passenger's side. In a nut shell, the practice of law is a Business and the expenses necessary to run it are substantial. Therefore, a certain amount of money must be produced by the attorney just to pay his/ her expenses. This money comes from fees paid for services rendered 95 percent of the time. (We will discuss some ways to increase your fees in a later chapter.) The expenses involved come around on a monthly basis, while, on the other hand, the fees paid do not. The paid fees are sporadic in nature and can drive a person crazy if he or she has no other source of income. Office rent, secretary pay, utilities, phone bills, cell phone charges, advertising, stationery, - amount to a substantial sum that must be generated on a month to month basis before the lawyer gets to keep *any* money for himself. This is a very bleak picture for the attorney just starting out in practice. If a person is used to getting a monthly paycheck then he usually cannot stand the financial pressure of going for months without getting a paycheck. Many times these individuals decide to just quit the practice of law.

<u>4) Bad Clients:</u>

This perpetual lack of money forces the attorney to take on criminal cases and heated divorce cases just to pay the rent. These usually result in the lawyer having to deal with an habitual liar who is a hardened criminal that tells him that he had better keep the subject out of jail or else. I have gone to court with criminal clients who said they didn't have any felonies and who, I thought, would get probation at their probation hearings only to find out that they had about 300 prior misdemeanors. My experience with criminal cases has been that I have *never* been appointed to represent a client who was innocent, and the lawyer is forced into negotiating with the D.A. based upon what the client **said** happened, only to be shown by the D.A. and the factual evidence that the client is a total liar and did in fact commit the crime. Criminal work on appointed cases, usually just boils down to trying to get the D.A. to lower the charge to get a better deal on the sentence, because of the overcrowding of the jails. If the State had plenty of jail capacity there would be very little criminal work available to do, based on my experience, because the D.A. would not have the added pressure to shorten the defendant's sentence for that particular crime.

With heated divorce cases, both sides **hate** each other and want to kill each other. When working with criminal cases, the victim and the perpetrator usually don't know each other and the perp is just trying to get some money to buy dope or whatever. Therefore, it's usually not an emotionally charged case. Whereas, with many divorce cases, the parties are so emotionally involved with each other that they will do completely childish things to try to hurt the other party. You, as their counsel, are, many times, reduced to playing these childish games on their level, and aiding and abetting your client in his/her efforts to use their children as a bargaining tool. Many times things become so silly that they are almost comical, but the parties hate each other so much that the emotions are too high to laugh.

5) I Feel Sick

When you become an attorney you will be responsible for all of your own insurance. Medical insurance alone can run $500 to $1500 per month if you have a family. I know a lawyer whose wife drives a school bus just so the family can have medical insurance. Don't get me wrong there's nothing wrong with being a school bus driver. I mean, after all, if it weren't for bus drivers there would be a lot of students walking to school. However, insurance issues from malpractice insurance to medical insurance to life insurance truely take a toll on the monthly expenses that a lawyer has to pay to stay successful, healthy, and protected.

Several of the referral services that provide leads on cases to attorneys require a certain level of malpractice insurance. All to often a new attorney overlooks the expense of insurance. Especially, if he has been employed in some other job where the insurance was all paid by his employer. One of my classmates in law school was a fireman in Birmingham. He, also, had four kids. After two years of attempting to practice law, he quit and went back to being a fireman because the expense of health insurance was just too prohibitive.

Sometimes the State Bar will refer cases to an attorney when a potential client calls the State Bar for a referral to an attorney in his Circuit. The state bar maintains a list of attorneys for case referrals. However, the State Bar requires a lawyer to have this minimun level of malpractice insurance to be included on the referral list. These are all expensive issues and must be addressed by all "new" attorneys. If the attorney has a family, the medical insurance expense alone is many times much more than the practice can bear for a new lawyer.

6) Student Loans:

This is a biggie. Imagine having to pay huge sums of money every month for a loan that you obtained to help you get a job that you now *hate!* How depressing does that sound? Yet, that is exactly the situation facing roughly 60-75 percent of the new attorneys just beginning to practice. Checking with the law schools in Alabama, it turns out for the school year ending in June 2004, that approximately 69% of the law school graduates had student loans that they obtained through their school's financial aid office or a bank. All of these students have some form of student loan to pay back when they graduate. The next question is "How much?" Well, at Jones Law School in Montgomery, the tuition is $18,500 per year; while at Cumberland Law School in Birmingham, the tuition runs about $24,700 per year. It follows that if the loan is just to pay the price of tuition, then, after three years the average total loan amount could run anywhere from $55,000 to $74,000 plus interest. This is quite a load to bear for someone just starting to practice with NO experience. We discussed this debt service issue in detail in Chapter 6.

Let me give you a good example of this burden. About five years ago, I was in the office of one of my local attorney friends discussing an upcoming case. He had been practicing for ten years at the time. While we were talking, he was sitting at his desk paying his monthly bills. He exclaimed to me as he finished writing one of the checks - "Well, I've got my student loan paid down to $42,000." I was flabbergasted. He had been paying on this student loan for ten years and still owed $42,000! If he were able to pay $1000 per month, he would still have five to six years before he would be free of that debt. Fifteen to thirty years of student loan payments - How enticing does that sound?

7) Personality Conflicts:

This one gets back into the psychology of the "job." A person's happiness is the result of many factors. And their job plays a major part in their happiness. Let's be objective for just a minute and examine what an attorney is up against. What profession has the highest rate of suicide among its members? Dentistry. The reasons behind that are many. First of all, everyone *hates* to go to the dentist. Even if their Dentist teaches their Sunday School Class and they've had a crush on him since ninth grade, they still hate going to see him for their dental appointment. Everyone does. Some more so than others, but nobody likes it. He is always having to encourage his patients to come see him, to floss, and to brush regularly. It seems that his job is always to *beg* people to do what they should do to take care of their teeth. Then, unfortunately, many people don't heed what he says and they wind up getting chronic gum disease and/or lose their teeth, and he feels really guilty about it. After all, they are *his* patients. Even when he does a good job, it still doesn't make his patients *like* to come to see him. Doctors are not much better. Almost every time a Doctor sees a patient it is because that person has a major problem. He doesn't get to see them at all when they are well. Unless, of course, it's for a checkup. But, generally, Doctors only get to see people when something serious is wrong with them. Lawyers are in a similar situation. The people who come to see lawyers always have a problem of some type. Sometimes the problem is serious. Sometimes it's critical. Sometimes it's beyond help. People have a tendency to ignore legal problems hoping they will go away. They, many times, go to see a lawyer as a last resort, only to find out that they have waited too long and there is nothing that can be done for them. Whether it's a divorce, an arrest, a car wreck, or whatever, they never come to the attorney unless they have a MAJOR problem. This is compounded by the fact that they are never objective about *their* situation. They feel like *their* case is very serious and that you, as the attorney, should devote 100% of your time to getting *their* case resolved to their satisfaction. They always feel that *their* case is unique. They feel this is MY case; it's my husband who's treating ME bad; it's MY car wreck; it's MY arrest and I'm innocent. I've had to remind many of my crying, whining divorce clients that it was *they*, and not I, who picked this individual to marry. When I do this they usually get pissed off because it makes them realize that THEY caused their own problem. It didn't just happen to them. That instead of being mad at him or me, maybe, they should be mad at themselves. They seem to not be able to ever see things objectively when it comes to *their case*. Once you begin to practice, you will realize that if you have 500 open case files in your file cabinets, then you have 500 people that you have signed up that have 500 major problems, and all 500 feel that you should devote *all* of your time to their case.

These are just some of the main factors that I have found that cause this *hate*, and these factors are not isolated in their nature and who they effect. Most attorneys will have to deal with some, if not all of these, in their initial practice if they don't have some other source of steady income. I was fortunate in my practice, because I had monthly retainer checks and hardware maintenance checks ongoing from my computer business. I, also, taught adjunct faculty classes for two local universities. Additionally, I taught management and systems seminars for area businesses. I was lucky. I haven't been forced to accept any of these "loser" cases, because I *needed* the money. Unfortunately, many of my classmates did not have that option and are now dissatisfied with their choice of careers. They wasted their time, money, effort, and in many cases even their family, to acquire an occupation that they now despise to perform on a daily basis.

Chapter 13

THINKING OUTSIDE THE BOX:
How to cultivate your practice.

"A wise man will make more opportunities than he finds."
Sir Francis Bacon

Once you've established your law practice, unless you have been taken in and given a "job" by a relative or friend attorney, you are going to need some help with getting good, new clients. Even, your LM won't be much help with this. What I'm talking about is *marketing yourself.* When my wife told my mother-in-law that I was going to law school, she replied "Why? Lawyers are a dime a dozen." For our area, that is true. I've already given you some statistics on that, but, with that said, do not despair because there will always be enough business for you, if you have the right attitude and know how to market yourself properly. Most attorneys know a lot about the law and usually something about political science, but very, very little about marketing - much less marketing themselves. Some of the things that will be discussed here might not apply to you, but most of it will. You need to hang onto this book and not let your fellow lawyers (your competition) see this chapter because they will use these hints to try to steal some of the market share from you.

Let's start with what NOT to do. As I mentioned earlier, one mistake that many attorneys make is to buy a big yellow pages ad. Some attorneys spend upwards of $1500 per month for a display ad. That's a lot of money when you are just starting out in practice. In our local yellow pages for '04-'05, attorneys had 20 pages of display ads. Eight of the display ads, are for attorneys from out of town - cities such as Birmingham and Gadsden. We have 156 attorneys in our county. These lawyers from these other circuits must think that 156 is not enough for someone from this county to pick a lawyer to handle their case. They spend big money to run ads in our yellow pages when the market here is already overly saturated. It is absolutely ridiculous. The lawyers from out of town who run these ads rotate, because they eventually see that virtually no business is generated from the ads from our Circuit and discontinue to run them after a year or two. The types of ads these lawyers run, and this includes even some of the local attorneys, are, also, ridiculous.

About 90% say -   We specialize in:
                  Personal injury
                  Auto Accident
                  Divorce
                  Criminal defense
                  DUI
                  Wills & estates
                  Social Security
                  Worker's Comp.
                  Wrongful death

So, basically, what their ads are saying is that they *specialize* in nine or ten areas. So just how *specialized* is that? Potential clients get the same impression from all fifty or so ads in there. After a time the impact of each ad is so diluted by the other ads that it becomes worthless. If you feel the urge to advertise you really should pick a different venue than the yellow pages. The attorneys that use that as their primary source of advertising usually change to some other form after a time. Another point about yellow pages advertising that could be well taken is that there are a few really fat, ugly lawyers here and they put their *picture* in their ad. How's that for poor marketing?

You may be asking yourself by now if I'm going to give any constructive tips or just complain about what everyone else is doing? Well, let's start by getting you to understand what's important and what's not from a marketing point of view. I have an MBA and I taught marketing for years for one of the local colleges. I'm sure this gave me an edge over the other attorneys that had never had any marketing.

First up, you need to begin by treating all of the clerks in the Circuit Clerk's office *special*. I started out not knowing just how much assistance the clerks could give me. But, you'll learn quickly that they are one of your most valuable resources. They can give you great advice on procedure and other things of a technical nature that you can use in your filings - advice you can even bill your clients for. After I began to learn the ropes of the Court House pecking order, I began to use it to my advantage. For instance, I would take every female clerk that worked in the clerk's office a small box of candy for Valentine's Day. I would, also, take them a box of Christmas candy at Christmas time and would always smile, be friendly and speak to each and every one of them. I would always have a pocket full of mints to hand out to everyone as I went through the Clerk's office. After a year or so, I began to get moved to the front of the line when filing anything. They could be waiting on a patron and see me come in the room. They would tell the person that they were helping "Hold on just a second," then come over to me and say "Hey, Phillip. What do you need, Honey?" By my third year in practice, I was the favorite Attorney of all the clerks. Now, that didn't cost a lot of money. Some of these presents I bought at the dollar store. But it was a very, very good investment. Another thing that will work to your advantage is to kiss up to all of the Judges' judicial assistants. After all, they are the ones to sort through the Judges' mail, motions, etcetera. They see to it that the most important things get moved to the top of his stack.

And I wanted to be sure that all of them thought that my filings should be placed on first priority. I gave these judicial assistants <u>bigger</u> boxes of Valentine candy and <u>bigger</u> Christmas presents. A very wise barrister once said "A good lawyer knows the Law. A great lawyer knows the Judge." And having the inside track to the Judge's attention comes much easier when you are a favorite with his judicial assistants and his Court Reporter.

------------------<>--------------------<>------------------

All Judges, from time to time, have cases in which they need to assign special counsel. I'm not talking about being on the indigent list for criminal cases and juvenile cases, but about civil cases where the County or State has need to sue someone or something. In indigent criminal cases, the attorney is paid the state's pre-set hourly fee, which I believe is presently $60.00 for in Court and $40.00 for out of Court work. And this indigent list consists of all attorneys in the County who signed up. So, the list is long and there are not many cases to go around. Therefore, not much revenue can be generated for your practice by being on this list. However, there are civil cases that occur from time to time, that the Judge will need to assign an independent third party counsel to handle. It could be a suit, special master, receiver, or whatever the case requires. Remember, the District Attorney's office handles the *criminal* cases in that Circuit. Hence, if you are appointed by the Judge to handle a civil case, you can charge your regular $150 hourly rate. See what a difference this makes. Plus, the work is usually much more pleasant than the indigent criminal work.

------------------<>--------------------<>------------------

Because of my background in Accounting and my thick skin, one of our Judges appointed me to be administrator for the closing of the *Community Action Agency* in our city. I have mentioned this case in a previous Chapter. I billed and was paid my normal hourly billing rate for all work accomplished on that case, which over a two and one-half year period amounted to over six figures. So, it's all in your perspective. The appointment to these cases is a direct result of the recommendation of the judicial assistant to the Judge that you be the one he picks, at least for the first time. Then if you do a fantastic job on the case, you'll be in line for more assignments of this nature. But it's important to recognize the role that the judicial assistant plays in the Judges assignments, etc. I would bet that there are dozens of Attorneys in my Circuit who don't even know that the Judges sometimes assign special counsel in some *civil* cases.

------------------<>-------------------<>------------------

Another tip - Always, and I mean always, keep some business cards in your shirt pocket. You will be asked legal questions in the supermarket or wherever you go and instead of just giving out *free* advice to someone on the street, give them a card and say "Call me and set up an appointment. I'll be happy to handle that for you." Another area that attorneys usually don't think about addressing is the CPAs who practice in your area. They are always having occasion to consult an attorney or have their clients consult an attorney. So, concentrate on taking them to lunch, out for a beer or whatever is necessary to get them to send some business your way. If you are going to play golf and you have a chance to be in a foursome with a CPA that you don't know yet, pick that foursome to play with instead of your usual buddies. Now, keep in mind, that if you have a tendency to throw your club after the ball and swear when you hit a bad slice, then perhaps you should just play with your buddies, but this is an easy way to network and broaden your exposure. Offer to speak at the Rotary luncheon or any local civic club on a current legal topic such as living wills. This always generates new clients. Volunteer to serve the sausage at the annual Kiwanis pancake breakfast. Offer to teach a seminar at your church on a week night. For instance, giving one at your church on "living wills," will precipitate Wills, Trusts, Power of Attorney - type business.

-------------------<>--------------------<>------------------

Begin to develop your expertise in an area of the law that interests you, such as, say, internet law, or any other area that suits your interest, and write articles or stories about that area for newsletters/publications. I, personally, write articles on technical subjects such as computers/internet matters for the Alabama State Bar *Addendum* newsletter. The addendum's editorial staff appreciates the contribution, and it is a tremendous way to gain exposure as a, so called, *expert* in that area. Your first reaction might be - "Well, just how do I do that?" And that's a good question. Say, for example, that internet law is your area of interest, you need to keep an eye out for CLE seminars on that subject. You can, also, spend some time at your local *Books-a-Million* store in their periodicals section, locating and buying any magazines that have articles on that subject. The internet is another good resource that you can utilize to explore this area. As I have stated previously, there are many excellent search engines out there that can provide you with a variety of ideas and information on your area of interest. I have had lawyers from other circuits refer clients to me on matters involving computer fraud and other technical issues, because of the articles I wrote. It can be any area you pick. It could be securities fraud or something like gift and estate tax - just chose something you already know a little bit about and build up your knowledge over time. Offer to be the speaker on this topic at the monthly County Bar luncheon. This will set you up for referrals from the other lawyers in your Circuit, who will now consider you an <u>expert</u> on this topic.

-------------------<>--------------------<>------------------

Develop a reputation for being a "bulldog" on Commercial account collections. *All* businesses have some accounts that are way behind in payment. Many times a letter from an attorney is all it takes to produce payment. Keep your CPA friends apprised of your collection efforts for other clients, and make sure that they think about you when they see that large figure in *Balance for Doubtful Accounts* on their client's financial statements. They know who needs collection help! Keep in mind that getting a client, even fifty cents on a dollar, sure beats nothing, which is what they are probably going to get otherwise. I, personally, provide commercial collection services for credit unions, garbage companies, and others.

------------------<>-------------------<>------------------

Always think outside the box. Use your imagination. The other attorneys in your circuit will cover all the mundane, routine cases, leaving you the ones that nobody else *thought* about. Let me give you some examples of thinking "outside the box." I represented a lady in a divorce. I, generally, only do uncontested divorces, but, I knew this lady (I'll call her Faye) and she was about forty years old and very ill. She had C.O.P.D., and she was married to what she called a scum-bag of a truck driver. I filed the divorce and he answered it. However, she could never get in touch with him for any negotiations because he was always on the road. She had accused him of staying with his girlfriend when he was home. The court date was set for a Friday afternoon and she showed up with her oxygen tank and walker. She had called the trucking company where he worked and they said he was gone to California. Sure enough, he failed to show. She had only been able to pay me fifty dollars so far, so I asked the Judge for a hefty sum for my attorney's fee. During trial, I asked the Judge for everything I could think of and he granted all of it against the defendant.(I'll call him "Sonny.") Well, about two months later, Faye passed away. I waited about three months and I called Sonny to ask what was his hold up on paying my fee. He stated that he had married his girlfriend, that she had four kids, and that one of them had asthma. But, that he would begin to pay what he could. So, about every month or two, I began to get a money order from him for $5. He was smart enough to not send a personal check. This went on for about a year and he had paid me $25 for one whole year. I called him and told him that it would be the year 2031 before the fee was fully paid at that rate. He said that was all he could afford and made me feel sorry for him. At this point, most attorneys would have said "Just forget it." Fast forward to the next January. My computer company (BSI) provided computer systems software and services for the company where Sonny worked. And they hired BSI to prepare their W2's for their employees that year. So, I instructed my computer tech to let me see the W2's for inspection before they were sent to the CPA's office. She did. And I did. I checked Sonny's W2. Well, guess what? He made more than $47,000 that year driving long haul. I went to the family court clerk's office the next day and got a certified copy of the divorce decree, carried it down stairs to the Circuit Clerk's office, and filed a garnishment on Sonny's wages with the trucking company. I got all of my fee within six weeks time.

-------------------<>-------------------<>-------------------

Another client owed me twelve hundred dollars for a criminal case that I took because this client's mother was a good friend. The client was a nineteen-year-old hairdresser. She had paid me some of the fee that I had agreed to take on a weekly payment installment because her mother was a close friend. But, she got laid off from her job. The payments stopped. I attempted to locate her place of employment for about two years, but she kept changing jobs every two to three months. Eventually, she signed up, along with her parents, for the PCB mass tort case that I was handling against Monsanto, because she had lived close to the plant. I charged everyone a $7.00 fee to double check their Social Security Number against the previous claimants who had already received settlement payments from the previous suits against Monsanto/Solutia. She paid her seven-dollar payment with a check. That was all I needed. I garnished her checking account. *Tip.* - Once you begin to practice, anytime a client pays you with a check for anything, always make a photocopy of the check, so that you will have their checking account number because you might need it later.

------------------<>--------------------<>------------------

Another good example of thinking outside the box occurred in the CAA case. As you will recall, the Judge appointed me to be the Receiver/Administrator for the court ordered shut down of our local Community Action Agency. He closed it because of financial mismanagement by the executive director. This was a large agency which at one time had more than 200 employees, and an annual budget of $9 million. An employee pension plan was involved. I was appointed to oversee the plan as well. At first, the plan assets could not be located. However, after some research I located the funds in two investment accounts set up by the former executive director as self appointed Trustee for the plan. It was a qualified ERISA plan and some of the former employees who were plan participants filed a suit in Federal Court in Birmingham when the Plan corpus could not be located, to try to enlist the Federal Court's power to force the former trustee to produce these funds. When I found the funds, the plan was worth about $ 636,000. After I became trustee, and managed the fund for 18 months while the shut down and law suits were ongoing, the plan grew to be worth over $ 1,151,000. The state paid my attorney fees for work on this case during this period. After seeing the fund perform so brilliantly for over a year under my supervision, I was speaking with one of our local bank investment officers one day in the bank's lobby. He asked if I would roll part of the fund into one of their investment portfolios. I asked what was the annual administrative/trustee fee for that. To which he replied "Generally, 2.5 to 3.0 percent." The leg work that I had been performing for the shut down was being paid by the state at my usual hourly rate. However, just as importantly, if not more so, was my custodial performance on the pension plan during this time. I mentioned this fact to the Judge and he agreed that a reasonable trustee fee should be paid for these duties. Upon my motion to the Court, I was paid over $ 50,000 out of the fund for this function.

--------------------<>--------------------<>------------------

One of my good friends is the general manager for a large local manufacturing company and he had a lady that worked in sales for his company that needed my assistance. She was the conservator for her mother who was in an insane asylum. It was time for the four year interim accounting of the Conservatorship, and she came to me to handle it for her. (I'll call her "Sally.") She knew of my accounting background from my friend. Her mother had been in this institution for nine years. During the process of my trying to assemble the data to file the accounting, her mother passed away. (I'll call her mother "Mom.") Well, Mom had a house that Sally was trying to maintain in one of our local subdivisions. The house was a three bedroom, one and a half bath dwelling with a nice backyard. However, it had been empty since Mom had been admitted to the institution, except for a couple of times that Sally had rented out the house for a few months. With the exception of this house, Mom had no assets, save her gowns and the other clothing she wore in the institution. The furniture had been sold or given away after Sally decided that Mom was never going to be able to leave the institution. The unexpected death of Sally's mother quickly changed the Conservator's interim accounting that we were doing into a *final* accounting. After the funeral, the final expenses, including the final statement from the mental hospital began to arrive. Mom had been receiving Medicare payments that were being paid directly to the hospital, but they didn't cover the total cost of the hospital's monthly charges. Sally brought the final bill from the institution to my office almost in tears.

It stated that Mom owed the hospital $197,000. She thought that she might have to pay this herself. I tried to explain to her that she (Sally) was not personally responsible for her mother's expenses, and that even though she was a good, honest person and didn't want to cheat the hospital out of any money, that she had not incurred these expenses and they were not her responsibility, but the responsibility of Mom's estate.

Keep in mind that most attorneys, at this point, would have told Sally that there wasn't much else that could be done, finished the final accounting, sent her a bill and let the hospital have the house. But, learn to think outside the box. Try to take a minute here and think about how you would have handled this case before continuing to read what I did. What would you do? Now, pay attention to what I did. Instead of putting the file back in the file cabinet and moving on to the next case, I began to consider the outside the box options to this. About a month of *thinking* about this case, and examining the many factors involved, I knew that everyone who went into that hospital was <u>crazy</u>. I, also, knew from just plain common sense that none of these people had any assets. Think about it. If they can't be responsible for their behavior, they can't be responsible for their finances. Any assets that they might have had before they went *crazy* have since been gobbled up by any relatives or associates left behind on the outside, and I knew that Mom would be viewed as no different from the rest. I took the following action. I called the mental hospital and found out who was the director of financial services for the institution which, incidently, is about 200 miles from Mom's hometown. Then, I called him and the conversation went something like this:

"Hello. Is this the financial director for the Hospital?"

"Yes, I'm Mr. _____, Business Manager."

"In that position, are you the one responsible for making any financial arrangements for settlement of past due accounts, or is someone else responsible for that function?"

"I'm the one who handles that and has the final say on any account settlements."

" Well, Mr._____, I'm Phillip Estes, an attorney from Anniston, and I'm calling regarding Mom's account with your hospital. Could you look at that account with me for a minute? "

"Be happy to. Just hold on a second while I pull up that account."

"Mom has a house over here that her daughter has been trying to take care of, and since the house will be going to your hospital to settle this bill, I wanted to tell you that you would have to come over here to the Probate Judge's office for the hearings on the final Conservatorship accounting. The only assets that Mom had was this house, and that will have to be transferred to your hospital as partial payment for the bill in question. And I will be calling you back with the time and date of the first hearing. Probate Judge Murray will be presiding over this matter."

"Whoa! Whoa! I don't need to get involved in that. The Probate Judges do these kinds of hearings all the time. He won't need me there will he? After all, can't you just get the Judge to settle it however you and he sees fit. I don't have to attend do I? After all, the State of Alabama is not in the real estate business, and we really don't want to get involved in this." (I knew he would say that.)

"Well, I'm, sorry but you won't have any choice since your institution will have to be the one to take title of the house. I'm sure the Judge will require you, as Business Manager, to attend all of these hearings to settle this final accounting." (I knew he wouldn't like that. This was going to be a 10 hour trip for him.)

"Now, just wait a minute. What kind of house is this anyhow?"

"Well, it's a three bedroom, one and a half bath house in an old subdivision down in Oxford - part brick and part frame - probably about 40 years old."

"Well, what do you think it would appraise for?"

"I don't know. I've never seen the house, and we haven't had it appraised yet. And it has been sitting there vacant for nine years, except for a few months that her daughter had it rented, so I imagine that it probably needs some infrastructure maintenance work."

"Well, what's your best guess as to what *you* think it's worth?"

"I don't know. I'm not familiar with that area and how the schools are or any other factors that would help dictate the price."

"Well, just guess for me would you please?" (He was getting frustrated with me.)

"Forty to fifty thousand, as a rough guess, provided no major air conditioning, plumbing, or other repairs are needed."

"Well, we don't want to have to mess with all this. Fixing it up. Selling it. After all, we're not in the real estate business. Does this daughter have any money?"

"I don't know. She might. I do know she works in a local textile mill." (Actually she was the sales manager.)

"Do you think she might have $30,000?"

"I don't know about that. Like I said, she works in a textile mill."

"Do you think she might have $25,000?"

"I don't know about that, either. But I think she might have $20,000."

"Well, you find out and if she can send us twenty thousand cash, we'll satisfy Mom's bill."

"I'll find out about that and get back to you by Friday. And I thank you for your time. Good bye."

"Good bye."

I called Sally and set up lunch for the next day at a local pizza parlor.

We met at noon. She was nervous. We both ordered the buffet and I began to try to put her at ease. I asked her if she had built up any equity in own personal residence. She said she had over eighty thousand in equity. I, then, asked her about her credit. She said that she had excellent credit. Then I broke the news to her about the deal that I had secured for her. She began to squeal, jumped up, ran around to my side of the table, and kissed me on the cheek. Everyone in the restaurant was staring at us. I gave her the name of an officer at the bank who had said he would love to handle the equity line for her. She borrowed the money. I prepared the release and sent it along with the $20,000 check to the business manager. The house appraised for $78,000 after she and her boyfriend painted it. She sold the house for $77,000 and she and her niece split the $57,000 left after she paid off the $20,000 loan. I would like to add at this point that she was very thankful for my work in this matter and rewarded me splendidly when she remitted my final fee. She called many times to thank me. And for about a year she told everybody that she saw what a great lawyer I was and proceeded to send me dozens of clients.

--------------------<>--------------------<>-------------------

I saved the best example that I have of "thinking outside the box" for last. About nine years ago, a local attorney named Donald Stewart filed a suit in our Circuit on behalf of 3,600 plaintiffs for damages due to exposure, contamination, and injury from polychlorinated byphenols (PCBs). These PCBs were manufactured in only two places in the United States - Anniston, AL and Sauget, IL. They were manufactured by Monsanto Chemical Co. at those plants. PCBs cause cancer and many other diseases in laboratory rats. The company made these chemicals from the 1930's to 1976, when the EPA banned their production. These chemicals were a good conductor of heat but would not conduct electricity, thereby making them seem ideal for huge electrical projects. GE and Westinghouse were two of the main customers for these materials. Some of the industrial waste and by products from the manufacturing process used in the making of these chemicals were dumped into Snow Creek which ran right by the plant. This creek ran all the way through town and down by the Mall in Oxford. It continued all the way to the Coosa River about thirty miles away. The high level of PCBs had, over time, made the fish in that river unsafe to eat. Warning signs began to spring up along the river bank warning people to not eat the fish. Some PCBs were dumped in a large landfill located just outside the plant fence, that flooded when it rained and caused these chemicals to run off into the local ground water. As a result the area surrounding the plant became highly toxic over time. And many of the residents living in the vicinity of the plant became ill because of this. The health problems caused by PCBs include, but are not limited to: acne, severe skin rash, thyroid problems, respiratory disease, heart problems, liver damage, etcetera. These chemicals cannot be broken down by the human body and therefore once they get in your system they are somewhat permanent. Some individuals' bodies can tolerate them better than others. Not unlike the diseases linked to smoking, some people can handle the effects better than others. So, not everyone who was exposed to PCBs got sick. But on the other hand, the medical problems caused by them might very well manifest themselves later as that person gets older.

Monsanto continued to produce these chemicals for many, many years after they found out through their own tests that PCBs were harmful to humans and the environment. There were numerous company memos that showed the company was just trying to keep it quiet and not let anyone, including the EPA and ADEM, find out about these harmful effects. These chemicals were inexpensive to make and were very, very profitable to the company. Monsanto would pay independent lab companies to run tests on PCBs and they would publish only the test results that appeared favorable to the company. All of the tests that showed the real dangers of these chemicals were kept secret and never given to the public. The cover up was company wide and enormous.

Donald Stewart associated several top ranking law firms, some from out of state, to help with this case. The case went on for years. There were write ups about it in publications ranging from *Forbes* to the *Wall Street Journal*. The trial began and liability was established against Monsanto. According to Court records, Stewart spent millions in expenses for expert witnesses. Pharmacia had bought Monsanto, several years before. And Monsanto had spun off Solutia, which now owns the Anniston plant site, just before these suits began to be filed. It was questioned whether this was done as a ploy on Monsanto's part to try to avoid liability. All three of these parties were initially, named in the original complaint. Solutia, subsequently, filed Chapter 11 bankruptcy. Monsanto hired several of the big law firms in Birmingham and St. Louis to represent their interests. Rumor has it, that at one time, one of these defense firms was on a $ 1,000,000 a month retainer. The case lasted for seven years before it was finally settled.

Paralleling that case, the EPA sued Monsanto/Solutia to force them to clean up the area surrounding the plant and its flood plain. Just prior to the time of the trial, Jerre Beasley's firm out of Montgomery began to sign up other plaintiffs from the area as well. Beasley filed that suit in Federal Court in Birmingham. They even associated Johnnie Cochran to fly into Anniston and address the issue at the City Conference Center on a Sunday afternoon. A total of about 18,000 people were signed as plaintiffs in this Federal suit. That, along with the other suit, represented almost 22,000 people, who were, simultaneously suing Monsanto for PCB contamination. Recall that the County only has 110,000 population. Well, the cases ran parallel for a while and were finally resolved when Monsanto agreed to settle the cases for $ 300 million each, in August of 2003. Some plaintiffs received awards of over $300,000 based upon the level of PCBs in their blood and how badly their land was contaminated. The progress of these cases was mentioned from time to time in the *Anniston Star*, and it was watched closely by the people living in the effected areas. The people in the *Beasley* case received an average of $ 16,666 less attorney fees and expenses, while the plaintiffs in the *Stewart* case received an average of $ 83,333 less attorney fees.

Once these plaintiffs began to receive their checks, there were a lot of new luxury cars that began appearing on the Anniston streets. It had been a long haul and many people never thought that the cases would amount to anything, because Monsanto kept telling everyone that PCBs weren't harmful. As a result of these suits being settled, occasionally a plaintiff who had signed up and received a big check would go to his next door neighbor and show off his big check. Needless to say, there were many native Annistonians who felt like

A Survival Guide

they were *left out* because they didn't bother to sign up. I would have individuals come up to me all the time and say "My neighbor got $18,000 from that PCB suit, and I didn't bother to sign up because Monsanto kept saying that PCBs wouldn't hurt me! Do you know any lawyers who are still handling any of these PCB cases?" I was reared and went to school about a mile from the Monsanto Plant. Everyone I knew from that area had been exposed to PBCs and my mother still lived out there by the plant. And her land had been rendered basically worthless by these chemicals. It seemed a shame that some of these poor people were left out of the settlement. But on the other hand they had the chance and thought it silly to sign up. These two cases were not the only cases that had been filed against Monsanto/Solutia. Some of the residents along the Coosa River, also, sued Monsanto/Solutia to force a clean up. These cases were expensive, time consuming, and extensive. Individuals kept asking me if I know any attorneys who were still taking PCB claims and unfortunately I did not. Then, one day I was driving home from Birmingham and it occurred to me - "Hey! I know a good lawyer who might take some PCB cases from these West Anniston residents! ME!" I wrote an ad and ran it in the *Anniston Star* the next Friday. It read as follows:

"MECHANICSVILLE/WELLBORN RESIDENTS"
If you lived or went to school in the Wellborn/Eulaton/Mechanicsville area, you MIGHT be eligible for damages from Monsanto due to PCB contamination. If you would like an application to see if you might be eligible please send a self addressed stamped envelope to:
Phillip Estes
P.O.Box 9999,
Anniston, AL   99999

Two days later I went to the Post Office to get my mail. I have a medium sized P.O. Box. When I checked my box there was a post office green card notice in there and that was all. I was extremely disappointed. When I went to the counter and gave the card to the mail clerk, he brought out a bushel basket full of mail for me! From that point forward, I signed up a total of 6,200 potential claimants against Monsanto. After blood tests and other screening, the eligible plaintiffs' cases have been filed in State and Federal Court and are presently ongoing against Monsanto.

------------------<>--------------------<>------------------

So learn to use your imagination. As you can see, *thinking outside the box* is more fun, pays better, and is usually less work than approaching your practice in the conventional manner. So work on it and I promise you will enjoy your practice by adhering to that philosophy.

So, in closing this chapter, go back to the first of this chapter and read Sir Francis Bacon's quote again!

Chapter 14

The Rewards

The return from your work must be the satisfaction which that work brings you and the world's need of that work.
William Edward Dubois

As I had previously mentioned in an earlier chapter, the reasons for individuals wanting to become attorneys vary widely - likewise, the rewards. By that I mean, the rewards are subjective and depend upon the person. That is one of the reasons behind the lack of satisfaction in this line of work. Some of the rewards that these individuals *thought* they would get from that "job" didn't materialize. One of the texts I used when teaching an *Organizational Behavior* course at one of the local colleges, listed the following elements given by a survey of employees as to what constitutes a "good" job:

Good working conditions
Good wages
Customer satisfaction
Job recognition
Job security
Interesting work
Promotions

Vacation time
Fringe benefits
Work Hours or schedule

This shows the wide range of things that people feel are important about their job, and what they want to get from their work place. A quick look at these items indicates that these same elements could apply to the' "job" of lawyer. After all, being an attorney will be your "job." If you are the *Ralph Nader* type, spearheading the legal fight to protect the environment might be reward enough for you. Furthermore, you might even volunteer to perform this work for free because of your unrequited love for the outdoors. So, money would not be your primary motivator for becoming an attorney. On the other hand, if you are the *Johnny Cochran* type and feel that the persecuted, prosecuted and misunderstood *O.J. Simpsons* of the world need representation, then perhaps your motivation might be job/name recognition, as well as monetary. The point is, the reasons that you chose to become an attorney will go a long way in defining the types of *rewards* that you would like to get from your work. However, if you are one of those poor souls that chose to become an attorney because you were so impressed with the job that *Ben Matlock* did when he was able to get the butler acquitted of that murder charge on that Wednesday night episode back in 1997, then it may be a while before you realize *any* rewards from your practice. Think about it, there may never be a butler in your town that gets charged with murder! So, you could go through your whole career and never feel as though you fulfilled your destiny!

------------------<>-------------------<>------------------

Law is a profession that does so many good things for mankind. If you are a lawyer who enjoys your work then the rewards of choosing that as your profession are *great*. There are many wrongs in the world and, if not for the pursuit of justice, there would be many more.

Furthermore, the pursuit of justice would be futile without Attorneys. I have friends who became CPAs and I have friends who became Doctors. There are many noble professions available to people in our great country. The job that, for the most part, would carry the most job satisfaction with it is, probably, minister. I mean, what could be more meaningful than helping to save someone's soul. But we can't all be ministers, so with that said, I'll try to explain why the profession of attorney is such a *noble* calling. An attorney is the only person who can keep an innocent person from spending his life in prison. He is, also, the only person who can make another individual treat you with the respect that you are due. There would be no "rule of law" without attorneys. There would be anarchy in the streets of America, without the stability that the rule of law gives us. Many attorneys want to help fight the injustice in the world, while others, simply, look forward to the challenge of a trial. A great feeling of self worth and job satisfaction should come from knowing that you are helping people who have major problems. Many of these individuals need the type of help that only a good lawyer can provide.

-------------------<>--------------------<>------------------

In examining the elements previously listed, we can better understand just exactly what "rewards" to expect from our job as an *Attorney* and relate that to our own individual ideas of job satisfaction. For an attorney it would read as follows:

1) Good working conditions: - nice office, desk job, air conditioned.

2) Good wages: - hourly wages as high or higher than any other occupation, except, maybe, Medical Doctor.

3) Customer satisfaction: - even lousy lawyers do a better job for their clients than those clients could have done alone.

4) Job recognition: - a job well done on a case doesn't go unnoticed and can even make the newspaper if it is a high profile case.

5) Job security: - as long as there are people who can't manage their finances or their relationships, there will be a need for lawyers' services.

6) Interesting work: - as you can imagine, the work is very interesting - it is never dull.

7) Promotions: - this one is tricky. About the only promotion you get is that the better you become at the practice of law, the more you can increase your hourly fee.

8) Vacation time: - tricky, as well. But you can take off as many weeks for vacation as your practice can afford. A very good aspect of this is that the vacation destinations are, generally, much better on an attorney's pay.

9) Fringe benefits: - aside from the *lawyer mystique* that you automatically acquire when you become one, you have to pay for all your own fringes

10) Work hours/schedule: - this is up to you, but the hours can be long at times. This one is tricky as well. There are several local lawyers that I know who had extremely *high maintenance* wives - big house on the mountain, new sports cars, beach condo, - and these attorneys had to work long, hard hours to keep their wives in the lifestyle to which they had become accustomed. They are all now divorced because their wives said that their husbands were neglecting them! So, be careful. Long hours are a two edged sword.

------------------<>--------------------<>------------------

Enough about the rewards, let's talk about the money. Show me the money. After all, it's like the old adage "Money talks, and Bullshit walks." Now, I'm not saying that all of these other rewards are bullshit. I'm just saying that all the other rewards will come if you have money. The *potential* to make a lot of money comes with becoming a lawyer, probably more so than any other profession.

Notice that I said "potential." For instance, if we performed a statistical analysis on the incomes of different occupations, there would be many millionaires on the list - heart surgeons, rock stars, oil men. The "potential" to make a million exists for such people as heart surgeons, but they have to make it over time. They get paid by the hour, just like the boy who works the counter at McDonalds. The doctor's hourly rate is higher but he is still on the clock, so to speak. Insurance agents get paid commissions for policies they have sold in the past, every time someone makes a premium payment. So, they earn money for past work. People who develop software have the potential to resell it over and over thereby making money from very inexpensive copies. These, of course, have the potential to make one wealthy, but to put this into perspective, the law is one of a very, very few jobs where people give you money just for telling them something. Think about that, we are consultants, counselors, lawyers, and therapists all rolled into one.

The one thing that sets the legal profession apart from all other professions is the opportunity available to you *on any given day* to become a millionaire. This is not to say that all attorneys are rich or that all attorneys will have a chance to become rich. I'm just saying that for the lawyer, the potential to become wealthy exists. After all, I have just spent the last three or four chapters talking about how some lawyers are having cash flow problems, or how their phone service was terminated due to non-payment, and other such tragic events. So, you need to understand that the practice of law is not a guarantee that you will become wealthy, but it is one of the very, very few occupations that affords you the opportunity to become wealthy on any given day. Occupational statistics probably would bear out that, on a percentage basis, a larger percentage of attorneys are millionaires than any of the other jobs available to an individual today. For example, an attorney can have bad cash flow problems and be about to shut his doors, only to have a client walk in whose wife has been killed in a tanker truck accident in which the driver of the truck was drinking when he ran a stop sign and caused the collision. The employee worked for one of the three big oil companies. Furthermore, the client's wife was only 34 years old, but made $106,000 a year as vice president of a local advertising agency. Now, I'm not saying that a case like this would always make the lawyer a millionaire, but I am saying that in order for this case to not make this lawyer a wealthy man, he would have to do something exceptionally stupid to screw the case up. Additionally, there would be a great deal of work involved with a case like this. However, when the dust settled, this attorney would be instantly wealthy when he received his percentage of the settlement check. Someone can get a job playing third base for the Atlanta Braves and become a millionaire but how many of those jobs are available. On the other hand, an automobile accident happens every 10 seconds in the U.S. So, your chance of getting at least one of these "home run" cases during your law career that has a big payoff is very good. Hand in hand with this wealth goes the heart warming feeling that you are helping someone who has been terribly wronged! Most of these type victims are treated like second class citizens by the insurance companies and are usually offered very low, often insulting, settlement options for their accidents. The insurance company adjusters feel that it is their job to see to it that they never pay anyone a *dime*. I had an accident case once where my lady client was sitting at a stop sign waiting on the traffic to clear so she could proceed. Another lady turned left in front of an on coming car which broadsided her and crashed that car into my client's car, thereby knocking my client's vehicle into a ditch. The letter that the insurance company wrote to my client offering settlement of $300.00 stated that they considered her partially responsible for the accident. In other words, they implied that she contributed to the wreck! Now, just how utterly insane is that proposition? She brought the case to me and I proceeded to obtain a good settlement for her, but these types of offers are what most victims of car accidents are having to deal with when they try to contend with the insurance companies without legal representation.

As you can see, the rewards for being an attorney come from within. The money is good if you think outside the box, and keep a good attitude. The cases will come. Knowing that you are helping someone truly in need, who cannot help themselves is reward enough most of the time. An attorney friend of mine, who is also a published author, once said "I would rather try a good case than to eat when I'm hungry." This is the type of attitude that keeps the legal profession from disintegrating under the enormous pressures that we have discussed in this book. And as long as that attitude can be maintained by myself and "you" if you have decided to become an attorney, then the profession will be fine and the world will be a better, safer, and more just place. Q.E.D.

Appendix A
A Typical Law School Curriculum

Tort I & II
Personal Property
Sales
Contracts I & II
Domestic Relations
Criminal Law
Legal Ethics
Legal Research I & II
Equity I & II
Agency & Partnership
Corporations
Real Property I & II
Evidence I & II
Court Speaking I & II
Legal Research III & IV
Conficts of Law
Insurance
Constitutional Law I & II
Statutory Rights & Remedies in Land
Bankruptcy
Secured Transactions

Criminal Procedure
Practice Court I & II
Bills & Notes I & II
Income Tax
Estate & Gift Tax
Civil Procedure I & II
Wills
Trusts
Intellectual Property
Practice Court III & IV